CANADIAN CRIMES & CAPERS

A Rogue's Gallery of Notorious Escapades

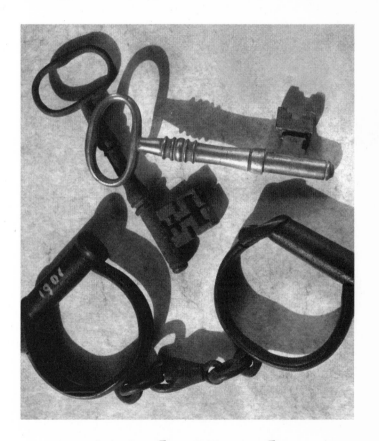

Angela Murphy

FOLK
LORE
PUBLISHING

The Publisher: Folklore Publishing
Website: www.folklorepublishing.com

Library and Archives Canada Cataloguing in Publication

Murphy, Angela, 1946–
    Canadian crimes & capers : a rogue's gallery of notorious escapades / Angela Murphy.

(Great Canadian stories)
Includes bibliographical references.
ISBN 1-894864-30-1

    1. Criminals—Canada—Biography. 2. Crime—Canada—History.
I. Title. II. Title: Canadian crimes and capers. III. Series.

HV6805.M87 2005   364.1'092'271   C2004-907062-2

Project Director: Faye Boer
Project Editor: Tom Monto
Production: Arlana Anderson-Hale, Linda Bolger
Cover: Courtesy of Sun Media Corporation

We acknowledge the support of the Alberta Foundation for the Arts for our publishing program.

PC: 5

Table of Contents

~x~

Dedication

Dedicated to my delightful, inspiring,
and fondly remembered friend Lee Cameron,
who passed away during the writing of this book

Acknowledgements

My gratitude and love goes out, as always, to my husband Peter, for his ongoing support and encouragement of my various and sundry dilettante pursuits, and to our daughter Sarah for always keeping alive the spirit of wonder and the power of stick-to-it-ness. To Faye Boer of Folklore Publishing for her belief in this project and for her expert guidance throughout; To my editor Tom Monto for his eagle eye and quick wit; To Neil Duboff and Carolyn Frost, barristers and solicitors, of Duboff, Edwards, Haight & Schachter of Winnipeg for invaluable assistance with legal terminology, and clarification on some subtleties of the criminal justice system; To friend, actor and fellow writer Stone Wallace for opening the door on an exciting new adventure; To my dear and patient women friends who often wait days for phone calls to be returned while I am "in writing mode"; And to my late aunt Angela Murphy Larkin, former San Diego, California journalist whose name I have appropriated for this book. I have no doubt that she is, at this very moment, enjoying a good chuckle over the tender irony implied.

Introduction

The chapters in this book are the tales of men and women who made conscious choices to go against the laws of our country. Although it was not the original intent to cast judgement for or against any of these real-life characters, I have no doubt that astute readers will be able to decipher the tone in which each chapter was written, whether in disgust, disdain, empathy or amusement.

Be that as it may, my sympathies lie completely with the victims of these crimes, not with the criminals who perpetrated them. In all cases, these criminals seemed to have more concern for themselves and for satisfying their own needs—whether material, social, or emotional—than for their victims. I have dealt with a narrow look at the broad spectrum of the criminal mind: from princes to pirates, from aristocrats to bureaucrats, from housemaids to hoodlums. If there is a common thread among these individuals, it is their failure to be concerned with the harm that resulted from their actions. Taking responsibility for the outcome of our behaviour is, ultimately, what separates us from lower life forms.

It is my sincere wish that this book does not appear as a celebration of crime or criminals. Nor do I wish it to appear as an utter condemnation of the individuals whose stories have been told within these pages. However, when they chose to break the law, with little thought for whom they hurt in the process, they forfeited their right to be free from public sanction. And it is likely not their wealth, status or personality for which they will be remembered. It will be their criminal behaviour.

Good or bad, their lives form part of the fabric that is Canada's history. As such, their stories need to be told. May their lives and how they led them teach us a little about what it takes to be truly human.

CHAPTER ONE

Bill Miner
Highfalutin' Highwayman
(1846–1913)

The good folks of Princeton, British Columbia could not believe their eyes. There was the dear old face of their lovely gentleman neighbour George W. Edwards plastered all over those nasty newspapers, and they were saying that he was a train robber! Why, he was no more a thief than the minister or the schoolteacher, and what's more, the children in the area loved him, flocking to his grand house to listen to his stories and have a glass of his fine lemonade.

They just couldn't believe this wealthy, grey-haired Southern gentleman (well, that's what he said he was) could be connected with thievery. Mind you, they had not heard of him before he arrived in their midst just as 1899 had turned over into the new century. And, he did seem to have an inordinate amount of money, claimed to be an inheritance from his dear departed Pappy. He also seemed to take an unusual number of sudden business trips to who knows where, and his likeness to the photos...It just couldn't be. Could it?

The man the good folks of Princeton, BC, knew as George W. Edwards was indeed a thief. The manners and style of the man born Ezra Allen Miner were not the vestige of a genteel past. They were cultivated by the quick-witted Miner as a way to get people to let down their guards before he made them hand over their treasures.

Although Miner told various versions of his life story and ancestry, his parents were neither fabulously wealthy nor Southern aristocrats. He was born on December 27, 1846, to Joseph and Harriet Miner, farmers who had settled in Michigan. The young Ezra Allen, who called himself Bill, was only 10 years old when his father died. Harriet and her three sons, along with several other families, migrated to a gold-mining town near Auburn, California. It was a hard life for a young woman who had no husband, but Harriet was good enough with her needlework to get a job as a seamstress. Although it does not appear that she was a trained schoolteacher, as Bill Miner later told people, she taught her sons manners and literacy skills that were well beyond what public school provided.

In 1864, 18-year-old Ezra Allen Miner legally changed his name to William Allen Miner and did a brief stint in the Union army. Leaving the army only one year later, he started a new life on the wrong side of the law. He committed robberies at gunpoint and knifepoint, horse-theft and stage-coach hold-ups. His profile included crimes committed in Colorado, California and Oregon. By the time the innocent residents of Princeton, BC met their kind-hearted, gentlemanly neighbour, he was already a hardened criminal and was known by several aliases.

In fact, by the time he rolled into their sleepy little town in early 1900, he had spent more than one-half of his 54 years doing hard time in San Quentin, the toughest prison in North America. He had served more than 33 years, with his first incarceration at 19 years of age. For his adult life, he had known little other than a prison home.

He settled well into the peaceful and friendly environment of the Canadian West. He loved to attend dance parties and soirées and was a favourite with the ladies. His refined manners and cultivated speech made him an attractive dance partner and a popular dinner guest. He was in great demand for social engagements and he attended whenever he could. Whenever, that is, he wasn't off in some distant location taking care of business. Little did his innocent friends know his business was crime. While living in Princeton, he continued to carry out robberies in his American homeland and was wanted by police in several states.

It wasn't until he decided to rob the Canadian Pacific Railway Company that he attracted the attention of Canadian authorities, the intrepid

Royal North-West Mounted Police. Joined by two accomplices with whom he had done several jobs in the U.S., 57-year-old Miner boarded an unguarded CPR train on September 10, 1904, as it pulled out of the junction at Mission, BC after taking on water. Armed and experienced, the bandits quickly took control of the situation. They instructed the engineer to separate the locomotive, baggage car and two small mail cars from the rest of the train and move them on to a siding.

There they went through the baggage and mail cars and left with close to $7000 in gold dust, nearly $1000 in cash and a bond worth $50,000. They made their getaway by rowboat across the Fraser River, then fled across the border near Matsqui, BC, on stolen horses.

Bill Miner resumed his genteel life in Princeton, thrilling the ladies with his wit and charm. He was so confident in his disguise and his ability to hoodwink people that he sometimes had fun at their expense. One Sunday morning, while scouting out Kamloops under the pretence of a business trip, he preached a sermon to an impressed congregation when the regular preacher failed to appear. He was never without money during that time, and it was likely that his ready cash further convinced people that he was who he said he was. All the while, Miner, with various associates, continued his life of crime.

On April 29, 1906, Bill Miner, the lower part of his face covered by a handkerchief, boarded a westbound train near Kamloops. He ordered the engineer to uncouple the engine and the first car from the rest of the train and to drive them to the next siding. When they slowed to a stop on the siding, his two accomplices quickly boarded and put the CPR employees under guard. Miner entered the train car, anticipating that it held a safe containing a large sum of money destined for San Francisco. The masked bandit had the shock of his life when told he had the wrong car. Miner and his cronies had mistakenly left the mail car containing the safe with the rest of the train. Instead, they had ordered the engineer to haul the baggage car. As luck would have it, the baggage car carried $40,000 in cash that day, but the irate robbers never found it. They jumped off the train and headed for the woods with a measly $15.50 in their hands. Unfortunately for Miner, his anger caused another problem that came back to haunt him. He became so angry when he realized his mistake that the handkerchief slipped off his face, giving the train engineer a good look at him.

Once the theft was reported and the robbery style was relayed to American authorities, it was clear that the polite, grey-haired, elderly robber was none other than Bill Miner, the fugitive they had been hunting for over six years. The efforts of the U.S. law enforcement agencies, the Royal North-West Mounted Police and the BC Provincial Police were combined, and a massive manhunt began, with a reward of $11,500 posted. The Bill Miner Gang, as it became known, was considered armed and dangerous and police were ordered to shoot-to-kill if they encountered the gang.

Assuming he would be unwelcome back in Princeton, Bill Miner never returned. Little did he know that he had become a hero of sorts. The people of the West hated the Canadian Pacific Railway Company, believing it to be a moneymaking venture for self-serving eastern capitalists who were insensitive to their need for agricultural land. When they heard that a man named Bill Miner had robbed these eastern crooks of thousands of dollars, they cheered.

Although Bill Miner would have been greeted with open arms by the public, he would have been met with handcuffs by the police. Miner and his buddies went into hiding. On May 14, 1906, the Mounties approached three men camping near Douglas Lake, asking them to identify themselves and state their business in the area. One of Miner's accomplices went for his gun, but the Mounties were too fast. The three criminals were apprehended and brought back to Kamloops. A day later, despite his insistence that he was George Edwards, Bill Miner's true identity was confirmed and he was charged with several counts of armed robbery. On June 1, 1906, he was found guilty and sentenced to life imprisonment in the New Westminster, BC penitentiary.

His charm stayed with him however. Shortly after he began his term of imprisonment, he was visited by a young woman named Catherine Bourke who was the daughter of the deputy warden as well as a Christian Good Samaritan. She was so convinced of Miner's piety and desire to reform that she convinced her father to give Miner freedom to move about and mingle with other prisoners. Relaxed security was what Miner wanted far more than salvation. On August 8, 1907, he was assigned to work in the open-air brickyard. At an opportune moment, he and three companions scurried under a hole in the fence and climbed over the outer wall to freedom.

He crossed the U.S.-Canada border and apparently retrieved some of the cash he'd stolen and buried. He lived well for three years south of the border, then, deciding he needed to restock his wallet, he robbed a train in Georgia in April 1911, lightening it by $60,000.

It was his last hold-up. He was caught, tried and convicted. Imprisoned at Millidgeville State Prison in Georgia, he escaped twice, but both times was recaptured. At the age of 65, Bill Miner was sent to prison for the last time. He died of acute gastritis at Millidgeville on September 2, 1913, wearing heavy leg chains. Even at the age of 66, as he lay dying, he refused to promise not to attempt another escape.

CHAPTER TWO

～✠～

The Black Donnellys
Fightin' Family

In Ontario in the 1800s, barn raisings were often the highlight of the summer. With neighbour helping neighbour, and nothing more for pay than a hot cup of tea, a few slugs of whiskey and a midday meal, barn raisers could expect a return favour when they were ready to build for themselves. No one in Biddulph Township predicted that such a wholesome and charitable event would be the catalyst for a storm of terror the likes of which the area had never experienced. No one, that is, but folks who had made the acquaintance of The Black Donnellys. They had been expecting it.

Jim Donnelly (1816–80) and his wife Johanna (1823–80) were in their early 20s when they left their home in County Tipperary, Ireland, in 1847 and settled near Lucan, 17 kilometres outside London, Ontario. Their goals were similar to those of their contemporaries: a place to raise a family and a piece of land to call their own. Their means of reaching that goal was a little unorthodox, but not unheard of in those tough times. They simply squatted on a piece of land that appealed to them.

When the person who held paper title to the land discovered the squatters, he made a few attempts to get rid of them, but Jim Donnelly and his wife were not about to be evicted. They flatly refused to leave it. Too intimidated by the pair to pursue the matter, the landowner stopped trying. He sold the land title to a man who was up for a fight, and the trouble began.

John Farrell, a big, burly former blacksmith, bought the property at a premium and immediately decided to straighten out the no-good squatters. But Jim Donnelly wasn't prepared to go quietly. In the eight years since he and Johanna had arrived in the area, they had been busy cutting and clearing and had built themselves a small but handsome log cabin with a fine garden out back. They had also been busy elsewhere. By the time John Farrell tried to evict them, the Donnellys had six sons. Jim Donnelly had a lot at stake.

Farrell's first visit to the Donnelly home turned out to be a humiliating affair. The big blacksmith strode onto the property with complete confidence in his fighting skill and his rights. He left considerably humbled. With Johanna holding a rifle on Farrell's companion, and the young

Donnelly brood cheering from the sidelines, Jim Donnelly not only beat Farrell senseless, but threatened to send him home in a pine box the next time Farrell showed his face around their farm.

Farrell went home and licked his wounded flesh and wounded pride, then appealed to the law of the land to rid him of his unwanted tenant. While deciding issues of ownership, the courts of the time recognized the importance of the amount of work an individual had put into a property. Clearly, the Donnellys had developed and worked the Farrell property to a far greater extent than either the past or the current owner. In a decision that was not unusual at the time, the squatters were legally awarded half of the 40-hectare farm they had hewed out of the wilderness. Farrell's attempt had backfired, and he was hopping mad.

Within days of the court ruling, Farrell began building a large house on the field within view of the Donnelly homestead. He and his cronies, not brave enough to confront their unwanted neighbours, made a great noise of unloading wood and shouting incendiary remarks across the levelled fields, with Farrell openly promising he would get rid of the Donnellys one way or another.

A subtle war raged for the next two years. Farrell and the Donnellys made accusations back and forth about burned outbuildings, stolen equipment and poisoned cows. Nothing was ever proven on either side, but Farrell did his best to poison the townspeople against the Donnellys. He was quick to run to the local watering holes to recount and embellish every item of dirt he could find about them.

With Farrell's mean tongue wagging at every opportunity, the unwelcome residents became known as The Black Donnellys, a term Farrell himself coined. Farrell was determined he would rid himself of the family that he felt was making a fool of him by their presence. He made that goal clear to any and all who would listen. Then came the fateful barn raising in June 1857.

A man to keep to himself, Jim Donnelly couldn't count many friends among the residents of Lucan. He could, however, always be counted on to show up at barn raisings, usually with one or more of his strapping young sons in tow. Unkind tongues, likely led by Farrell, wagged that Donnelly was only there for the free food and drink. But it is more likely that healthy and hard-working Jim simply understood the toll it took to work the land and knew help was needed by all those who didn't have the strong hands he did to eke out an existence from the harsh Canadian landscape.

So, Jim Donnelly arrived at the barn raising site, this time, in the company of his second son William (1845–97). William, who was 13 at the time had been born with a club-foot. Handsome

and healthy, he was a quiet teenager who usually kept to himself.

The Donnelly father was drinking a little
more than usual that day and sat down to rest
in the heat of the afternoon. John Farrell, par-
tially drunk and hostile as usual, saw a chance
to exercise his sadistic streak. With Papa
Donnelly dozing in the shade, Farrell taunted
young William, making fun of his club-foot and
surmising what sin his mother must have committed to cause such a defect. William bore the
insults silently for a while, going on with his
work. After more insults, though, William had
had enough. He shouted at Farrell to keep
his big ugly mouth shut and went back to his
hammering.

A satisfied look crossed Farrell's face, and he
lunged at the boy. But the sound of his son's voice
had awakened Jim Donnelly, and he was only one
stride behind Farrell. He spun Farrell around, and
the other man's fist connected with his face. The
punch knocked Donnelly to the ground. Donnelly
threw a few punches, but Farrell threw more than
just punches. Witnesses claimed that, at one point,
Farrell threw his axe at Donnelly, narrowly missing his head. Donnelly, not up to his usual fighting
form because of the whiskey he'd consumed, fell
once more. He struggled to his feet, this time with
an iron bar in his hand. He lunged at his attacker,
delivering what turned out to be a fatal blow to
Farrell's head.

Donnelly, suddenly sober, could see Farrell was dying. He knew his life was worth nothing if he depended on witnesses to support a claim of self-defence. He made for his horse and galloped off as bystanders gaped after him, still in shock after witnessing the attack.

Jim Donnelly raced home, stopping only long enough to tell Johanna what had happened, and to get some food to keep him going while hiding out. He sprinted out the back door and disappeared into the woods behind the house.

For the next year, posses scoured the landscape and watched the Donnelly house, but Jim Donnelly had seemingly vanished into thin air. It wasn't until Johanna showed up in town visibly pregnant a year later that neighbours and the law were certain Jim had not gone far. It was said that Johanna was so ugly she couldn't have won a beauty contest even if she was the only contestant. Jim Donnelly had to be the father, and the search for him tightened.

Realizing it was just a matter of time before he was caught, Jim Donnelly decided he was safer in the hands of the law than with a mob set on vengeance. In early spring of 1858, he turned himself in after almost one year hiding out on his own property, sleeping in the barn and spending days working in the fields disguised as his burly wife.

After a brief and widely publicized trial, Jim Donnelly was found guilty. Sentenced to hang,

Donnelly was relieved when the sentence was commuted to seven years in prison. Those seven years were to change the entire culture of Lucan and the surrounding areas. Already known for its violence, it soon became one of the bloodiest regions in all of Canada.

It was rumoured that Johanna was the more aggressive of the couple and her more reasonable husband kept her wild ways in check. Her leadership of the family during her husband's imprisonment validated the rumour. Johanna had eight youngsters to care for when she was left on her own: 17-year-old James (1842–77), 14-year-old William (1845–97), 12-year-old John (1847–80), 10-year-old Patrick (1849–1914), nine-year-old Michael (1850–79), six-year-old Robert (1853–1911), five-year-old Thomas (1854–80), and baby Jennie (1858–1917). Johanna raised them like a snarly, wounded mother bear. With a lovely baby daughter to round out the seven boys, Johanna kept her brood close to home. But she made it clear to them on a daily basis that they should take no nonsense from anyone. There were bad feelings in the community toward the Donnellys, and their schoolmates often taunted and bullied the Donnelly children. The badgering made the Donnelly boys more insular and bitter than before, and they regularly fought at school and in the neighbourhood.

As the boys grew into men, there was yet another reason for their neighbours to hate them. The children, it seems, had inherited their good looks from their handsome father. All tall, dark, athletic and dashing, the older boys got plenty of attention from local young females and plenty of jealous and protective responses from local males.

A spate of accidents occurred in early 1860. Mysterious barn burnings were the start, and they all occurred on the properties of men who had testified against Jim Donnelly. It was not long before rumours began to circulate in the district, fuelled by the Donnelly brood's failure to take the accusations seriously. The first time an officer of the law visited the Donnelly place to check on their alibis for the time of a bad fire, he left with more wounded than just his pride. The Donnelly boys beat him soundly and sent him off with a stern warning not to return. Subsequent visits by other constables faced the same disdain. The mysterious incidents continued.

In 1863, local happenings were no longer just mysterious—they were downright terrifying. Barn burning continued, but this was overshadowed by pet poisonings, highway robberies, cattle rustling and livestock mutilations. Rumour had it that the four eldest Donnelly boys were responsible. But no proof was ever found to pin the incidents on them, and they continued to remain at large, courting any girl they wished and sticking together against their adversaries.

There seemed no end to the misery the Donnellys caused their long-suffering neighbours. Not only were the boys handsome and brave, but they won practically every event in local sports field days. Year after year, they went home many dollars richer than when they had arrived. And, year after year, their list of enemies grew.

There was great rejoicing in the Donnelly household when father Jim was finally released from prison in autumn of 1865. As William played his fiddle, and the younger Donnellys danced together around the fireplace, neighbours huddled in their homes wondering what rowdy marauding would take place in the interests of celebration. They didn't wait long.

With their father back home, the Donnelly boys launched into a series of reprisals against all who had challenged them or reported their misdeeds. If anything, Jim Donnelly's presence made the Donnelly gang even more fearsome. Not a person in the county stood up to them and their reign of terror continued for the next several years.

No one denied that the Donnellys worked hard at whatever they did. In spring of 1872, the two oldest Donnelly boys bought out the stagecoach line where they worked as drivers. The only competition they had was an old man who was soon due to retire. The Donnellys thought their success was assured. Unfortunately, a younger man named Flannigan bought out the old man. Flannigan, respected in the county, took no time at all to establish his coach line as more than enough competition for the Donnellys. They responded with a serious business miscalculation.

Convinced that price slashing would ruin Flannigan, they were surprised when their actions had just the opposite effect. By 1875, the Donnellys were boycotted by all but a few intrepid souls. Despite their hard work and the comfort and punctual efficiency of their coaches, their family's reputation undermined the business. The Donnelly boys were on the verge of bankruptcy when the prospering Flannigan met with some suspicious bad fortune.

One morning, Flannigan discovered his coaches sawed into pieces, his tack sliced to ribbons and his horses badly savaged. He raised a hue and cry that brought a gang of men to march, in retribution, on the Donnelly farm. But it was not to be, at least not the way they had planned it.

The vigilantes never had a chance to aim their rifles. As the 30-odd heavily armed men converged on the little log cabin, the Donnellys attacked. Flannigan and his men later claimed that somehow they seemed outnumbered: that the Donnellys, all seven boys and their aging parents erupted from the house, screaming and laughing wildly, brandishing farm implements. The family broke up the vigilantes in record time and sent them scurrying away, bloody and bruised.

Then in the late 1870s, three events occurred that showed the Donnellys were weakening. In March 1877, a fire broke out at the Donnelly stable, killing their carriage horse and destroying the handsome coach. A few short weeks later, James Jr. mysteriously became ill. Although nursed at home by his loving and attentive mother, James Jr. died on May 15. He was 35. Although the cause of his death was reported as pneumonia, rumour had it that James died of lead poisoning from bullets lodged in his body after an attack by hooded riders just days before he died. Johanna and Jim were devastated, and the Donnellys set out on a rampage that put fear into anyone who had crossed James during his short life.

A third event, in September 1879 that began as nothing more serious than a missing cow, was the beginning of the end for the Donnellys. A mob of over 40 men swarmed the Donnelly property on suspicion that the missing cow had made its way, with their help, to the Donnelly herd. Both Jim and Johanna were in their 60s, white-haired and worn from a life of hard work, and Jim with crippling arthritis. Finding the two old folks at home alone, the mob of cowards became brave.

After tying up the two elderly Donnellys, the mob rampaged through the tidy home, breaking everything in sight. They pulled pictures off walls and smashed them; they ripped down curtains from every window and broke the windows for good measure. They knocked over chairs, sofas and a large china cabinet, leaving its contents in shards on the floor. They spilled the contents of Johanna's pantry and hacked the kitchen table and chairs to splinters. By the time the mob left, not one window, not one piece of furniture or china was left intact. The missing cow that had started the raid was found in a field on her owner's property, but no one bothered to go back to the Donnelly farm to clean up or to apologize.

The Donnellys brought action against the men who were responsible, but the case was thrown out of court when the 40 upstanding citizens produced false alibis for one another. With the law clearly not on their side, the Donnelly off-spring retaliated for the attack on their aging parents with tried-and-true methods. Burnings, beating and burglaries were heaped on the area once again.

Throughout the remainder of the 1870s, a rash of crimes went through Biddulph Township that made what came before look like child's play. During the next few years, all of the Donnellys except for Patrick and little Jennie spent time in court. John got three months for assault; Tom was in prison for two months for brawling; William and John were charged with arson but the charges were dropped. In the spring of 1878,

Robert was sentenced to two years for shooting at a police constable. Various other charges ranging from fighting to robbery to public drunkenness were thrown at the Donnellys. Some of them stuck; some of them didn't.

The coming of a new decade signalled a change in the continuing saga of the Black Donnellys. Fed up with their lawlessness, local residents formed a secret society calling themselves the Biddulph Vigilance Committee. Whatever else they pretended to be, they were vigilantes, formed for the purpose of ridding Biddulph Township of the clan named Donnelly. As history showed, they were willing to do it any way they could.

One fall evening in 1879, 29-year-old Michael Donnelly, who was living in St. Thomas, Ontario, was having a drink at a pub in neighbouring Waterford, about 100 kilometres outside Lucan. He witnessed a patron abusing a dog that had wandered into the bar. Michael shouted at the man to leave the animal alone. The man, joined by a group of friends, told Michael to mind his own business. Michael found himself surrounded by hostile drunken men who knew they had one of the infamous Donnelly boys in their midst. The standoff erupted into a brawl, and only minutes after he had opened his mouth to defend the dog, Michael Donnelly lay on the floor of the saloon, dead from a knife wound to the groin.

No one was ever charged with the crime, and it was rumoured, though never substantiated, that the men in the pub were members in good standing of the Biddulph Vigilance Committee. With a second son dead, and no one paying for it, the Donnellys were heartbroken and out-raged. They rode through the region under cover of darkness and burned and pillaged. Soon folks were afraid to leave their houses after dark.

On February 3, 1880, just after 10:00 PM, 60 members of the Biddulph Vigilance Committee met at the Cedar Swamp Schoolhouse, their usual meeting place. They were brought together by a recently hired constable, James Carroll. Carroll selected five men to stand beside him as group leaders: John Kennedy, Martin McLaughlin, James Ryder, Thomas Ryder, and John Purtell. All 60 men were extremely agitated. They stood around in small groups, taking long swigs from hip flasks and quart bottles of rye whiskey. As they drank, the men were handed small slips of paper. They all knew the drill. Half of the slips were blank. Half of them were marked with a large black "X." A few tense moments later, the 27 men who had drawn blank chits left for home, with the warning never to divulge any-thing about the meeting. Whether they were disappointed or relieved, no one will ever know. The 30 remaining men surrounded James Carroll, drank quantities of whiskey and made plans for what would be the bloodiest night of the century.

Just after 1:00 AM on February 4, the liquored-up mob, armed with pick-axes, shovels, pitch-forks and clubs, moved stealthily toward the darkened farmhouse and the soundly sleeping Donnelly family. Inside the log cabin were the two old folks, Jim and Johanna, and their son, Tom, 26. Bridget, Jim's 21-year-old niece who was visiting from Ireland, was also in the house, as well as an 11-year-old neighbour boy named Johnny Connor, who was helping out on the Donnelly farm. Johnny Connor, who scrambled behind a curtain when he heard the frenzied mob attack, was the only witness to the massacre that must have given him nightmares the rest of his life. And a bloody massacre it was.

As Tom Donnelly opened the front door, groggily peering into the darkness beyond, James Carroll barged into the room and hand-cuffed him. Moments later, the same fate met Jim when he appeared from an upstairs bed-room. As Bridget and Johanna came down the stairs to find out what was going on, Carroll hollered through the door to the waiting mob. The cursing, drunken horde surged through the doorway, weapons held high overhead. The Donnellys gave good accounts of themselves, but they were no match for the bloodthirsty vigilantes. Old Jim, handcuffed from the outset, kicked and fought to the end, almost beating three men to death. Badly outnumbered, he was beaten senseless and fell to the floor. It wasn't enough for the vigilantes. One of the crazed men raised his axe high in the air and brought its sharp blade down with a thud, severing Jim's head from his mangled body.

Meanwhile, Johanna and Bridget were hunted from room to room in the darkness. Johanna put up a valiant fight, swinging a flat-iron at her attackers. She was beaten to death, then given several hundred more blows until her face was unrecognizable as anything that had ever been human. Bridget, totally innocent of any wrongdoing, was not spared. The mob pursued her to a second-floor bedroom, where they caught her and dragged her down the stairs by her heels, banging her head mercilessly on every step on the way down. At the foot of the stairs, they clubbed her to death.

Young Tom was the last to die, and it is no surprise that he lasted so long. Tom early on had gained a reputation as the finest fighter in the county. This time he fought for his life. He kicked and whirled and lashed out with his manacled hands and almost made it out the door when someone threw a pitchfork that lodged deep into his back. The crazed mob dragged him back from where he fell, still breathing, into the kitchen. There they ripped and slashed at him until his body was little more than bits of sinew and crushed bone. In a brutal act of hatred, one of the men chopped Tom's head from his mutilated corpse.

As the crazed and blood-soaked men cheered and congratulated one another on a job well done, the terrified Johnny Connor scrambled under a bed. He ran for his life after he smelled coal-oil which the mob poured throughout the house. As Johnny ran across the pitch-black fields, faster than he ever ran before, he turned back to see the house ablaze and the frenzied gang outside cheering. But their job wasn't finished.

With only five men remaining who weren't sickened by their acts of horror, James Carroll proceeded to the farm of William Donnelly. What the marauders did not know was that John Donnelly was spending the night with his brother and sister-in-law. At 3:00 AM, it was John, awakened from his sleep in the downstairs bedroom, who opened the door to the loud knocks. Without waiting to see who showed his face, the mob opened fire and filled John Donnelly with 30 shots, then turned and fled, congratulating one another on having killed the devil cripple.

An investigation was launched, and arrests were made based solely on the unwavering testimony of little Johnny Connor. Although he tried, the defence attorney could not poke any holes in his eyewitness account, even after relentless cross-examination. Nevertheless, those who lived through the previous 30 years in Biddulph Township were able to predict the outcome. Perhaps they even prayed for it.

Almost one year after the horrific attack on the Donnelly family, the jury returned a verdict of not guilty for the six leaders. The town promptly held a reception in their honour.

The remaining Donnellys faded into obscurity. William and his wife moved away from Lucan and did not return until they were transported in their coffins, to be buried in the family plot alongside their murdered relations. Jennie, married and living in nearby London, never returned to her ancestral farm, the site of the massacre. Robert, who had been serving time in prison the night his family was massacred, worked in different locations after his release. His last known job was as a night clerk in a hotel in London, Ontario.

Patrick, the quietest of the clan, spent the rest of his days roaming the country from one coast to the other, returning to Lucan on only six occasions: for the funerals of the six men who were responsible for the massacre. As each of the coffins was lowered into the earth, Patrick uttered the same phrase in a loud and clear voice that no doubt sent shivers through the mourners: "There goes another of the bastards to hell!"

Many folks claimed the Black Donnellys were the most evil family of miscreants who ever lived and got only what was coming to them. Others, perhaps sobered by the horrible attack on the family, claimed the Donnellys had been scapegoats for a town in which lawlessness was a way of life. They believed the Donnellys were wrongly blamed for everything bad that happened over a 30-year period in Biddulph Township.

The legend lives on. It is said that the ghosts of the slaughtered Donnellys can be heard, wailing like banshees through the larch trees of Lucan, waiting for the right moment to punish the descendants of the men who murdered them in cold blood.

CHAPTER THREE

Ken Leishman
Plundering Pilot
(1931–1980*)

Airplanes seemed like the answer to a dream for poor prairie kid Ken Leishman. On the 1950s Canadian Prairies, the country boy turned entrepreneur flew into rural counties carrying his cargo of kitchenware, then flew off with his pockets full of money. He graduated to holding up banks in the late '50s, flying in and out of Toronto where he began robbing enough money to live the kind of life he wanted. A major gold shipment was next. An airplane was his getaway vehicle of choice. It seemed only natural that the last time anyone saw Ken Leishman, he was flying off into the afternoon sky.

Ken Leishman was born in Holland, Manitoba, into a family that, even by 1930s standards, was considered dysfunctional. His parents eloped when they were teenagers, and his father, Norman, was a hard-drinking drifter whose major source of

---

* The date Ken Leishman was declared officially dead.

income was government relief. Ken's early life consisted of travelling around various small southern Manitoba towns from one cheap motel or apartment to the next, while his mother, Irene, worked at any job she could find. After a few years, she couldn't provide for Ken any longer and sent him off to live with a succession of farm relatives.

Ken was good-natured and polite, but school wasn't for him. He quit at the age of 14 without finishing grade seven and without impressing people with his work ethic or his grades. He spent a short time working as a butcher's apprentice in Treherne, but he hated the dirty, smelly work.

Just when Ken was planning his next move, his father Norman showed up. Norman and Irene had divorced a few years before, and Ken hadn't seen his father for a long time. He was impressed with Norman's flashy clothes and big car. It was obvious to Ken his father was doing well in the elevator business in Winnipeg. When Norman offered Ken a job as his assistant, Ken didn't hesitate to accept.

In Winnipeg, Ken took on a new business-man's look. He grew a thin moustache that added to his 16 years. He was tall and good-looking, and he had a big smile and an easy-going manner. Best of all, he liked his job. His father had put him to work repairing elevators, and Ken took to the tasks immediately, finding the mechanics easy to master. He liked living in the big city and, even though the pay was minimal, it was more money than he'd ever had.

Two years later, still feeling like he had the world, and most of the answers, at his fingertips, he met pretty, red-haired Elva. He immediately decided that Elva was his kind of girl. They began dating and he was glad to be able to show off to her. He talked to her about his thriving elevator business and the plans for expansion he and his associate had. Elva was impressed enough to accept him when he surprised her with a ring just before Christmas 1949. They set the date for February 1950, and that was when Ken started to worry.

His job had been enough to impress Elva, but Ken doubted if it paid enough to support them. They found a small, unfurnished apartment they could afford but did not have enough money to buy furniture for their new place. Ken's luck stepped in again. Just as he finished cleaning an elevator in Genser's furniture warehouse, he discovered that he'd accidentally been locked in the building. It was not quite 6:00 in the evening, but all the lights were off, and the office doors closed. Ken spent a few minutes in awestruck silence. He and Elva needed furniture, and here he was, surrounded by it. He called out a few times to make sure he was alone, then set to work.

Checking the delivery door, he found that it opened easily and didn't set off any alarms. He sprinted across the street and phoned a delivery

truck service. Pretending to be an employee of
Genser's, he told the dispatcher he needed an
immediate pick-up, then raced back to the warehouse and quickly picked out pieces he thought
they'd need: a bed, a kitchen suite, a sofa, a chair,
lamps and two end-tables. It wasn't exactly the
furniture he would have chosen if he had time to
browse, but it had to do. Elva was proud of Ken
for being such a good shopper. He told her it had
been a real steal.

By March, Elva was pregnant, and Ken realized they would soon need baby furniture. He
made another elevator service call to Genser's
warehouse, timing his work to finish, as it had
with the last job, after closing time. This time
though, he wasn't so lucky. When he opened the
delivery door expecting to find the truck he'd
called, it was the police who greeted him.

The furniture was picked up and returned to
Genser's. Ken was charged with both thefts and
sentenced to nine months in provincial jail.
Released after four months, Ken was placed on
parole. With an empty apartment, a wife and a
new baby to support, he needed a job.

After nearly two months without work, Ken
finally landed a job as a combine serviceman/sales-
man for Machine Industries of Winnipeg. Driving
his junky old car over rutted dirt roads through
small towns of Manitoba, Saskatchewan and
Alberta, Ken felt a freedom he'd never felt before.
He enjoyed dropping in on friendly farmers eager

to see this cheerful and talkative young city fellow who seemed to be able to fix just about anything that went wrong with their combines. But once the harsh prairie winter hit, the bloom wore off that job.

Soon, Ken began to complain about the driving, the roads, the weather, and the distances. Sometimes there were 60 or 70 kilometres between customers, and his old car often broke down, making Ken late for his service calls. He often faced hostile farmers frantically waiting for repairs so they could continue their harvest. Ken got the bright idea that flying to his customers would be a much better idea than depending on the old car that was due to be retired anyway.

He bought a small, old Aeronea for $1000 from the Winnipeg Flying Club and signed up for flying lessons. In spring of 1952, with only five hours of flying experience, no licence and no hesitation about flying solo, Ken Leishman was back to his regular territory. Only now he was making service calls by air. The job was great fun. He loved the attention he got from the farmers and their families as he swooped in out of nowhere, fixed their machinery and disappeared again into the wide, prairie sky. Then, in September 1952 as he landed in Winnipeg after a particularly good run, he was arrested and charged with flying without a licence.

He probably could have weathered the suspended sentence and the financial setback of the $5000 fine if only business had continued as it had been. It didn't. Machine Industries closed down and sold their factory to Bristol Aerospace, manufacturers of fighter planes. Ken was hired as an assembly line supervisor for the new owners. The company was about to bid on some sensitive defence department contracts and was required to make security checks on all employees. Only six weeks into his job, Ken was let go because of his criminal record. At 23, with three children and a fourth on the way, he was out of work again.

He brooded for a number of weeks. Then an ad caught his eye. Next thing Elva knew, her husband was a commission salesman of luxury stainless steel cookware, flying his wares on the route he'd staked out with the farm machinery. The farmers welcomed him back. So did their wives. Stuck, as most of them were, more than a day's drive from the nearest department store, they loved this flying cookware man. He made more sales and more money in one month than he could if he'd worked day and night at Bristol.

By 1957, Ken was making about $10,000 a year, which was good pay in those days. It was enough for him to afford a shiny Cadillac and a new plane, a three-seater Stinson. That summer, he began to spend lavishly on gifts and fancy dining. He also began to establish a reputation as a con artist.

He honed his skill and smoothed out any rough edges by mimicking big shots that he met. He was in love with the excitement of being on the edge, knowing that one slip, and a sale would be lost. He was in love with himself for being able to talk people out of their hard-earned cash for a set of ordinary cooking pots. He was in love with life.

However, in the fall, the cookware company went out of business, and the bottom fell out of Ken's confidence and his bank account. He had several very bad weeks, then got a job selling executive jets for a while. He and Elva now had five children to raise, but business was tough since few people in Manitoba could afford personal aircraft. The days were bad. The nights were worse.

Shortly after deciding to accept that things would not get better, Ken had a vivid dream. He had been robbing a bank, and he'd been enjoying it. The dream was like a sign, pointing to a new way of life for Ken Leishman. He began looking forward to more lucrative employment.

Christmas was approaching, and Ken wanted Elva and the kids to have a good one. Although he still had his planes parked at the Winnipeg Flying Club, and his Cadillac parked at their River Heights home, his bank accounts were at an all-time low. It was time to put his plans into action. On December 16, 1957, Ken Leishman boarded a flight to Toronto on a trumped-up business trip. He was travelling real economy class this time on a return ticket purchased with $200 borrowed from a neighbour. Airport security was in its infancy, and he went easily through

check-in and boarding, armed with a grin and a
.22 calibre automatic pistol.

Once in Toronto, Leishman shifted into big businessman mode. A nice suit, a big smile, a briefcase
and, of course, the gun were the only props he
needed. The next day, he sauntered into the
Toronto Dominion Bank at Yonge and Albert
Streets and identified himself as Mr. Gair, a Buffalo
businessman with an interesting proposal. He was
ushered ceremoniously into the manager's office.
A few minutes later, the two walked to the teller
as Leishman pressed the hidden gun into the manager's side. The teller, assuming this chatty,
friendly guy was a friend of the manager's,
handed over $10,000 to cover the cheque he'd
been given. Leishman walked the manager out
the door of the bank and halfway down the
block. He shook the manager's hand and wished
him Merry Christmas then dashed around the
corner and took off in his waiting rental car. He
drove to Union Station on Bay Street and mailed
his locked briefcase, loaded with the cash and his
revolver, to his home in Winnipeg. Then he
drove, in bouncy good spirits, to the Toronto
Airport to catch his flight home.

The following day the briefcase arrived, and
Leishman spent the next few days buying fancy
gifts for Elva and the kids, and paying something
towards a few of the debts he had accumulated
with his fancy lifestyle. Except for his disappoint-
ment at not seeing splashy news coverage about

the fabulous bank robbery he had committed, Leishman was feeling like a big shot again.

One of the Christmas gifts he gave his family that year was a trip to Texas by plane—his plane. He jammed all seven of them into the small three-seater Stinson, defying all regulations and putting his whole family at risk.

While in Texas, he met several Texans who owned their own planes, and many more who thought Canada was a fisherman's paradise. On the way back to Canada, he realized that the distance from the southern states to Canada wasn't all that far. He decided he would open a fishing lodge near Kenora, Ontario, then offer fly-in fishing holidays. He figured the Americans would eat it up.

Soaring over the vast Canadian Shield area later, he found a suitable location for the lodge, and the land was available for a 99-year lease. With his typical lack of practicality, he hadn't planned how he would pay for the property or the building. He knew he wouldn't be able to complete the project alone, and the people he approached as potential partners wanted some control over their investment. Leishman would not accept their terms. He went ahead anyway, hiring local aboriginal workers and buying building materials on credit. By spring, he owed nearly $20,000 for the fly-in lodge, and his credit had dried up. At that rate, he would never have it finished in time for fishing season. It looked like he would have to return to robbing banks.

The second heist in March 1958 was planned exactly the same way the first one had been: a commercial flight to Toronto and a quick meeting with the bank manager where Leishman showed his gun and demanded money. But this time, the Bank of Commerce manager wasn't quite so willing. He jumped up and charged for his office door, shouting for someone to call the police.

Leishman realized the game was up and made for the door himself, but a middle-aged woman stuck out her foot and tripped him. Leishman sprawled to the floor, dropping his gun. A bespectacled clergyman who was just entering the bank kicked the gun out of Leishman's reach. Within seconds, the police arrived and quickly handcuffed the suddenly sheepish robber. The residents of Toronto were tougher than Leishman had counted on.

He was charged with one robbery, and if he'd kept his big mouth shut, it would have stayed at that. Instead, showing a personality trait that caused him trouble time and again, he bragged about the December job to the policeman guarding him. On April 17, 1958, Ken Leishman was sentenced to 12 years for two counts of robbery. At the time his now-defunct fishing lodge should have opened, he was beginning his new life as

The Flying Bandit, from the inside of Headingley
Provincial Jail on the outskirts of Winnipeg.

While in Headingley, Leishman followed all the
game rules for winning parole. He volunteered for
jobs, smiled a lot and was friendly to the guards.
Just before Christmas 1961, the role he'd per-
fected paid off. He was paroled at the age of 30,
after serving only 44 months of his sentence.

During his imprisonment, Leishman's involvement with the prison debate team led him to meet
Harry Backlin, a young University of Manitoba
law student, who was working with the team.
They hit it off right away. After Leishman's release,
Backlin helped the ex-con to line up a few jobs.
Leishman spent the next four years moving from
one sales job to another, always hoping for a big
break that would make him rich, but never quite
making it.

At a small get-together one night, Leishman
was with Backlin and a few other guys. They
were all complaining about being low on cash.
One of the group mentioned to Leishman that
holding up the gold shipments from Red Lake
was the solution to their money woes. Leishman
showed interest, and the man gave him what
details he knew.

Leishman learned that a couple of times a
month, Transair shipped gold bricks by DC-3
from the mine in Red Lake to Winnipeg. From
Winnipeg, they were transferred to Air Canada

and flown to Ottawa for delivery to the Royal
Canadian Mint. The idea caught Ken's interest.
He did some research on gold at the library and
dropped in at the Winnipeg Airport to scout out
the Transair facilities, waiting until a Transair
flight landed so he could see how the ground-
crew worked.

For the next few weeks, he hung around the
airport. As a pilot himself, he was on speaking
terms with a lot of the airport crew. A few of
them were interested in the time he spent in
prison, but no one seemed curious about why he
was hanging around. Mostly, they just assumed
he was missing the old Winnipeg Flying Club
social life. With his way clear, Leishman learned
all about freight capacity of the DC-3, Transair
flight schedules for Red Lake, Air Canada freight
transfer protocols, and the location of police at
various times of day. He even watched one Red
Lake gold shipment being unloaded just to make
sure. Then he applied for a passport. He figured
the job was going to be a cinch, and he wanted to
put distance between himself and the scene. But
he knew he would need help. And he knew just
where to go for it.

Leishman convinced Harry Backlin to join him,
and the consummate salesman got together the
best team of salesmen he could find: John Berry,
a 26-year old Tupperware salesman who had
worked with Ken selling cookware and two
Ukrainian brothers—Rick Grenkow, another

cookware salesman and Paul Grenkow, a vacuum cleaner salesman. They were planning to be rich, and this time, they wouldn't even need a sales pitch...well, all except for Ken Leishman. He had already talked the others into doing the job in a way that would get him the major portion of the heist. Harry Backlin's role was minimal, even though he was promised half of the take. He lent Leishman enough money to pay each of the other accomplices $4000 in advance and $2000 each after the job was done. The big sales leader calculated that his own net profit would be over a quarter of a million dollars. He had picked his sales team well.

On March 1, 1966, Leishman and his group were ready for their big strike. When the targeted flight landed just before 10:00 PM in Winnipeg, John Berry and Rick Grenkow were waiting at the landing strip dressed in mock Air Canada freight handler uniforms. They produced a forged waybill giving them authority to transfer the gold bricks from the plane into the stolen Air Canada truck that was waiting next to the runway. Accepting the waybill without hesitation, the flight crew then proceeded to help the two crooks load the gold into the truck, all 12 crates of it. Grenkow and Berry thanked the crew, and drove to the Air Canada parking lot where they loaded the gold into a Ford convertible they had waiting there. The next stop was a few blocks away where Leishman was waiting in his station wagon. They transferred the gold into the station wagon and drove off in the much-lightened convertible.

Leishman drove the weighed-down station wagon to Backlin's house in Riverview and unloaded the gold one more time. Backlin and his wife were away for two weeks as planned, and Backlin's mother-in-law was house-sitting. Leishman told the older woman that he was delivering some moose meat for Backlin. She promptly sent him to the basement where a grinning Leishman piled all but one of the gold bars into the freezer, stuffing it in among the packages of frozen peas and chicken wings. Leishman couldn't resist the temptation to open one of the boxes. The gold sat there, smooth and gleaming with its own power. Leishman decided to keep one of the bars for himself. He figured it had all been his idea, after all.

The crooks hung around Winnipeg in various locations, as newspapers all over the country blared headlines of the robbery. At the same time, a bad snowstorm crept in from the northwest, and by March 4, three days after the robbery, the city had ground to a halt. Leishman went back to Backlin's house to move the gold again, this time to a rented meat locker. When Leishman got to Backlin's place, he encountered two new developments. The mother-in-law reported a nice young man answering John Berry's description had taken away one of the packages the night before. Secondly, the snow was so bad that Leishman knew he wouldn't make it to the meat locker without getting stuck. He needed to move the gold again, but this time he just dumped it in Backlin's backyard. Within minutes, the 10 remaining gold bars were hidden under piles of drifting, blowing snow. A perfect hiding place, Leishman thought.

But police were on Leishman's trail. They monitored some phone conversations and knew that Leishman had just received his passport. They staked out commercial flights to the Orient and all small plane activity for hundreds of kilometres around. Within a few days, they located the gold under the snow banks at Backlin's house and soon rounded up the gang. Leishman, smug as always, was arrested on the runway in Vancouver, as he sat waiting for take-off on a commercial flight heading for Hong Kong.

Knowing the group's penchant for talking too much, police placed a skilled undercover RCMP officer, Corporal Allen Richards, in the cells with them. Within a few hours, the crooks had given specific details about how they had planned and carried out the heist. Leishman even crowed about how stupid his accomplices and the police were. He bragged that he would never be convicted.

On March 18, Leishman and the others were charged with theft and conspiracy to steal $383, 497, and in May were sent to Headingley Provincial Jail to await sentencing. Ken Leishman, 34, had bragged his way into prison once again.

Six months later, Ken was still in Headingley and still convinced he was too smart to be kept behind bars. He concocted a plan to break out and to take with him as many other prisoners as he could. Most of the prisoners were too close to parole to jeopardize their chances with him. It was a good decision on their part. When the breakout happened, nine men were foolish enough to follow him, and six of them were picked up that same night. Leishman and the remaining three were arrested on September 3. They had gotten as far as Gary, Indiana, after hijacking a car, stealing a plane and flying across the border. Leishman was in custody once again.

On October 30, 1966, he broke out of the Vaughn Street detention centre but was only on the loose for a few hours before he was picked up and put away again. At his trial in November, lawyers and spectators were shocked when Leishman was given a 12-year sentence. Many felt it was far too light. But Ken Leishman had already taken too much of the public's time and attention, and no appeal was launched. He was released in May 1974, after serving less than eight years.

After his release, he and Elva moved to Sioux Lookout, Ontario, and then to Red Lake, where the gold he had stolen originated. The Leishmans opened a gift shop and clothing store and were successful at it. According to reports, the Flying Bandit was unaccountably well-received in town.

In 1978, he was elected president of the Red Lake Chamber of Commerce, and later that year, ran for reeve but lost. Leishman also started flying again and worked as a relief pilot for Sabourin Airways.

On December 14, 1979, he piloted a twin Piper Aztec transporting a nurse and her patient from Sandy Lake to Thunder Bay. Just minutes after prelanding contact with the Thunder Bay control tower, Leishman's plane disappeared from radar. He was never seen again.

Rescue units were sent out from Trenton, Ontario. It wasn't until four months later, on May 3, 1980 that wreckage of the Piper Aztec was located. Nothing to indicate what happened to Leishman or his passengers was found. Also, not found was the three-kilo chunk that Leishman sawed off one of the gold bricks before they were recovered by police. That little chunk of gold would be worth nearly $120,000 today.

Was Ken Leishman really a brilliant, daring and romantic Robin Hood hero, or just another greedy crook who counted on being too smart to get caught?

CHAPTER FOUR

Hilda Blake
Homicidal Housemaid
(1878–1899)

Brandon, Manitoba. July 5, 1899

Mrs. Mary Lane mixed a jug of sweetened lemonade. It was ready to be carried out into the shady yard where her four small children and a few of their young friends were about to have a tea party. Little did Mrs. Lane know that her housemaid, Hilda Blake, was waiting for her chance to fetch the loaded pistol from her room. Minutes later, pregnant 32- year-old Mary Lane staggered from the house with a gunshot wound through the lung. She died only a few metres from the terrified children, in a pool of her own blood.

Emily Hilda Blake was born in Chedgrave, England, to a working-class family. Orphaned at the age of nine, she was sent to a grim workhouse. A year later, under the British Poor Law, the girl, who was known as Hilda, was slated for assisted emigration to Canada, along with a brother. The children were met in Canada by a religious and prosperous farm couple, Letitia and A.P. (Alfred) Stewart of Kola, Manitoba. The Stewarts had themselves emigrated to Canada seven years earlier to the small community north of Brandon.

Like some 80,000 other pauper orphans, or "home children," the Blake youngsters were expected to become part of the labour force of the family who accepted them in return for education, room and board.

Although the Stewarts were respected members of the community and well-off financially, they had difficulty accepting two foreign orphans into their family that already had five children from the widowed Mrs. Stewart's first marriage.

Little is known of the details, but Hilda ran away more than once from the farm, returning each time to a less-forgiving environment. About two years after arriving in Kola, Hilda ran away again, this time to the neighbouring Rex farm. Mrs. Mary Rex, a widow with grown children who helped out on her farm, was not on good terms with the Stewarts. Whether out of anger towards the Stewarts or from genuine compassion, Mrs. Rex welcomed the seemingly undernourished and unhappy girl into her home. This widened the gap between the two neighbouring families even further.

Hilda complained that Mrs. Stewart had been mean to her and wanted her dead. She claimed the woman had sent her out in the cold to walk to nearby Elkhorn with parting words to the effect that she hoped she would freeze to death.

When the Stewarts found out where Hilda was, they took Mrs. Rex to court, charging her with kidnapping. Mary Rex was sent to county jail for a brief period before her case came to court. She was acquitted, and shortly after, on Hilda's urging, applied to become Hilda's legal guardian. The guardianship was approved on April 18, 1889. Hilda was 11 years old.

The fact that Hilda now legally belonged to the Rex household didn't prevent the Stewarts from continuing in their attempts to bring her back. One day while Hilda was out herding cattle, the two elder Stewart stepsons convinced her to return once more to the Stewart farm. A short time later, Hilda changed her story of mistreatment at their hands. She wrote a letter of appeal to the courts contradicting her earlier contention that she had been unhappy in the Stewart home. In what the newspapers later described as artfulness, Hilda claimed that she had been well treated, well fed and had been given proper and beneficial religious and educational training at the Stewart farm. The culprit appeared to be Mrs. Rex, who, Hilda now reported, had treated her as nothing more than a servant. Mary Rex lost guardianship, and Hilda was once again returned to the Stewart family. It was not long before she ran away again. This time the Stewarts gave up trying to keep her at home. At 14 years of age, she was effectively on her own in the world.

Life likely would have been far different for Hilda, if she had stayed in the Stewart household. A poor immigrant orphan female in the late 1800s was only one step on the social scale above a prostitute. Of the tens of thousands of these girl orphans who were in western Canada at that time, many were so thankful to have a warm place to sleep and food to eat that they rarely complained about what were often unpleasant and sometimes dangerous circumstances. Placed without proper supervision or follow-up in homes where their presence was barely tolerated, these girls often suffered humiliation and sexual, physical and emotional abuse at the hands of ignorant and self-serving guardians and their families.

To be fair, many of the families who took in "home children" did so out of the goodness of their hearts and from a true sense of charity. Most of the children raised in these homes matured into solid, contributing members of Canadian society. In other placements, however, orphans were often scarred for life, either from the devastating circumstances they were in before arriving in Canada or from inappropriate placement once they got here. These unfortunate creatures sometimes fell into destitution or turned to crime.

By the time Hilda was 20 years old, she had worked in an unknown number of households. She was rebellious and wilful, and it can be assumed that not all of these placements were successful. Although she had adopted a less hostile attitude as she approached her teens, she never quite accepted the role society gave her. Many people she met thought she put on airs and had a pretentious and arrogant attitude that was at odds with her position in life. These characteristics did not endear her to many, and she could count few friends. In addition to being arrogant, Hilda Blake was also a liar.

Some time after leaving the Stewart household in 1892, she began using the alias Hilda Clark and passing herself off as a trained nurse. The name change may have been an attempt to start over or to cover up some indiscretion in one of her previous employments. During this time, she kept up correspondence with Mrs. Stewart. In the letters, Hilda claimed she had completed nursing training and was on her way back to England to seek employment as a nurse. It was rumoured that Hilda, also at that time, claimed responsibility for the death of Mrs. Stewart's 23-year-old son Robert Singer, who had died in 1894 of an apparent suicide. The claim was never followed up, but Hilda was already establishing herself as someone of questionable character. It would soon get worse.

In 1896, the 11-month-old infant son of Mary and Robert Crozier of Aikenside, Manitoba, died while he was alone in Hilda's care. The death was not registered until two days later, with the cause of death listed as "la grippe." A short time later, the baby's mother had a nervous breakdown, and there were rumours that it was because the family decided to cover up Hilda's involvement in the death.

Over the next few years, Hilda was able to find employment in various domestic positions in the Winnipeg area, and finally in Brandon. It was in Brandon in 1898 that Hilda, reverting once more to her birth name, was hired by Robert Lane and his family.

Robert Lane was a handsome and well-built man of 36 when he decided he could afford a domestic servant. A staunch Methodist originally from Ontario, Robert Lane was successful in every way that mattered to Victorian-era Brandonites. He was well mannered, well spoken, went to church regularly, was a caring husband and father, and was successful in business. A veteran of Boulton's Mounted Infantry in the Riel Rebellion, he had a prosperous drayman business in Brandon.

Robert's wife, Mary, was also highly regarded in Brandon society, but it wasn't only because her husband was successful. Mary Robinson Lane came from a well-connected family in Binscarth, Manitoba, with roots alleged to be in the British gentry. Mrs. Lane was a stay-at-home mom and delighted in caring for her four children. She was a kind and affectionate mother, a loyal and devoted wife, and was known as a generous and helpful friend to those in need. Mrs. Lane was active in her church, St. Matthews Anglican, where she helped to raise $14,000 for a new church building. In 1895, she helped found the Brandon Local Council of Women.

The Lanes were prosperous, but as is the usual story, prosperous at some cost to family life. Robert's business interests frequently took him out of the province and left an already busy Mrs. Lane to take care of the house and four small children. In 1898, when Hilda went to work for them, the Lanes had four children: Thomas, five; Edith, four; Mary, three; and Evelyn, one. Mrs. Lane was overjoyed when she found out that a young and energetic girl would be there around the clock to help her. She welcomed the pretty, fair-haired, blue-eyed 20-year-old Hilda into her home on July 15, 1898. Little did she know of the hostile ambition that was seething within this young woman.

The residence that welcomed Hilda Blake was a smart, comfortable two-storey home at 333 Tenth Street in one of Brandon's upper-class neighbourhoods. The Lanes had all the amenities available to families at the time: electric lights, a coal furnace, running water and indoor plumbing. Hilda's room was a standard servant's room, 2.5 metres by 4 metres, with a small closet, an iron bed, a chair and a washstand with a mirror. Hilda was housed in the room at the top of the stairs so that she could get up early in the morning to light the fire in the kitchen stove and make breakfast without disturbing the home's other occupants. As the only servant, Hilda was responsible for all the major and minor household duties, which included making meals, caring for the children, doing the laundry and all the house cleaning. Her workday usually ended once she had seen to the children's bedtime and cleaned the kitchen. In spring and fall, extra work was required, for carpets and draperies had to be aired or cleaned, and walls and windows scrubbed.

As the wife of a busy businessman, Mary Lane was expected to do a certain amount of entertaining, either at dinner parties or at informal social gatherings at which a light meal would be served. On these occasions, Hilda was required to prepare the meal, to serve and then to clean up afterwards. All of this was in addition to her usual duties.

Hilda Blake was a healthy young woman, and she took to the tasks well. She was fond of the Lane children, who adored her, and she was pleasant and helpful to her employers. She was also aware that her life as a servant in Canada was several steps above what it was to her counterparts back home in Britain. There she would likely have had to share a room with one or two other young women, used a servant's entrance, eaten from a separate, inferior menu and never, under any circumstances, be permitted any familiarity with her employers. In Canada, things were a bit more relaxed. It still wasn't good enough for Hilda.

Every day she saw Mary Lane, only 10 years older but with every privilege her class permitted. Mrs. Lane had stylish clothes, a grand home, beautiful children, a leisurely lifestyle, and what galled Hilda the most, a handsome husband. For Hilda, working and living so closely with this woman only heightened the differences between them, differences that Hilda refused to accept.

Hilda's wish to be something more than a servant became a fervent goal, and much of the goal she had set her sights on was the product of her self-delusion coupled with an overripe imagination. The self-delusion no doubt came from the middle name she carried. Her mother had named her Emily Hilda Beauchamp Blake. The name Beauchamp was the surname of the family the Blakes worked for at one time as tenant farmers. There was never any mention that Hilda might be the illegitimate child of the master, but the name nevertheless might have fuelled the young orphan's desire to "be someone." Her arrogance certainly suggested she wanted people to believe she was someone other than who she was.

To add to her delusions, Hilda was an insatiable reader of popular romantic novels. While Mrs. Lane was fashioning clothing for herself, her children and her servant and making curtains and bed linens to beautify her home, Hilda read novels.

While Mrs. Lane studied the latest edition of the Purity Flour cookbook for ideas for nourishing and delicious meals for her family and referred to Grandma Nichols' Household Guide for tips on decorating her home and conducting herself as a lady, Hilda read novels.

Her favourites were Sir Walter Scott and Charles Dickens, although she also enjoyed shorter works like Charlotte Brontë's *Jane Eyre* and Thomas Hardy's *Tess of the D'Ubervilles*. She read about heroes and heroines and knights in shining armour. Many of the novels she read featured protagonists the young servant girl could identify with. Characters such as Tess, or Nancy from *Oliver Twist*, were working-class girls just like Hilda. Just like Hilda, they aspired to something more. And just like Hilda, some of them were willing to kill to get it.

After Hilda had been with the Lane family for almost a year, two events occurred in the spring of 1899 that may have set the wheels in motion for Hilda to commit murder.

In May, Mary Lane travelled to Birtle to visit her parents, leaving her children and husband in Hilda's care. Hilda must have felt as if her dream had come true. While Mrs. Lane was away, Hilda was the one who served Robert Lane and his family their meals, tucked the children into bed, and kept company with the family in the evenings as if she were the wife and mother. Her later behaviour suggests that during this time that spring, Hilda also kept Robert Lane company in his bed.

As Hilda's infatuation with her employer grew, so did her ambition to share in his lifestyle. When Mrs. Lane returned, Hilda's dream came apart.

Within days, a second incident occurred that gave Hilda hope for deliverance. The local paper reported that a former employer of Hilda's had died of pneumonia at the age of 37. Hilda suddenly realized that even young wives can die. It was then that she began to plan how she would become the next Mrs. Robert Lane.

She started stockpiling quantities of laudanum, an opium-based painkiller, in her room. Hilda later testified that she intended to commit suicide with this sleeping potion, but changed her mind. The lawyers for the prosecution maintained that she intended to poison Mrs. Lane. She continued to serve her mistress, to cater to the needs of the Lane children and to display an attitude of calm acceptance of her situation.

Then, on June 20, perhaps concerned that the laudanum was neither of sufficient quantity nor fast-working enough for what she had in mind, she bought a gun. On a visit to Winnipeg on one of her afternoons off, she went to a gun shop where she bought an inexpensive .32 calibre American bulldog revolver for $3 and a box of bullets for 60 cents. She went home and hid the loaded revolver in her room, waiting for the right moment to put her plan into action.

A short while later, Hilda was forced to wonder whether the opportunity would ever come. Just three days after she purchased the gun, Robert Lane was injured when the dray in which he was riding was tipped by the sudden movement of a spooked horse. Lane suffered a fractured rib and was forced to take bed rest for several days. When he was ready to go back to work, the situation changed again. The older Lane boy was home from school on summer holidays, and the house was busier than ever.

A "welcome summer" tea party was planned for Wednesday, July 5, for the Lane children and their friends. Lane would not be home for several hours, and Mrs. Lane would be distracted with details for the party. Hilda saw this as her opportunity.

It was just before 4:00 on that beautiful prairie summer day, with temperatures sitting at a comfortable 21°C. The children were outside, seated around a child-sized table that had been decorated with a fancy cloth and set with some of Mrs. Lane's everyday china. The four Lane children had invited several their little friends to join them. They were waiting patiently for the tea party that Mrs. Lane had promised them, anticipating what lovely cool drinks she might serve for the occasion.

Inside the house, Mrs. Lane, pregnant with her fifth child, was busy at a tedious task that had likely been delayed because of her husband's convalescence. She was taking down the heavy damask curtains in the parlour and putting up the lighter ones she used in summer. She instructed Hilda to leave her ironing to prepare a small tray of bread and butter, and to take it out to the children, along with some fresh lemonade. Hilda stopped ironing, but instead of preparing the tray, she went upstairs to her room and returned with the fully loaded revolver. She slipped the revolver into her apron pocket and walked slowly into the parlour as Mrs. Lane eased herself down from the stepladder.

As Mrs. Lane turned, Hilda stepped forward and kissed her. Mrs. Lane stepped back, surprised at the uncharacteristic and inappropriate display of affection. It was then that she saw the gun. Hilda smiled and slowly raised her arm. She pointed the gun toward Mrs. Lane's head and fired. They were only a few steps apart when Hilda fired the first shot, but somehow she missed. Mrs. Lane turned and tried to escape into the hall, but she was slow, perhaps because of her pregnancy or because she just could not believe what was happening. When Hilda fired again, Mrs. Lane was no more than a couple of arm lengths away. The second shot went through her back, piercing her lung and lodging just above her heart.

Mrs. Lane cried out, "Hilda, I'm burning!" as she stumbled, screaming, out her front door and onto the sidewalk. She managed only a few steps, then collapsed to the ground in a pool of her own blood, her children near enough to hear her screams.

Hilda came outside a few minutes later with a cold cloth and began wiping the woman's face. By this time, several neighbours had gathered. They called for a doctor and carried Mrs. Lane inside her house, but she was already dead.

Hilda had her audience, and the second part of her plan began. She claimed that a tramp had come to the door and had been angered when Mrs. Lane refused to feed him without getting work out of him. Hilda, the only witness, claimed that the man had shot her mistress as she herself looked on helplessly. The neighbours seemed satisfied. The police were not.

Although a massive manhunt began for the fictitious tramp, details of her story did not fit for the investigators. The gun was found where Hilda had hidden it, beneath a barrel in the lane. Police Chief James Kircaldy, who led the investigation, re-enacted the crime as Hilda had reported it, but it was clear that the young woman was lying. The day following the funeral, Kircaldy arrested Hilda Blake, charging her with the murder.

Within days, Hilda confessed to the murder, at first claiming it was an act of sudden jealous rage. But to the jury, her purchase of the gun indicated that the attack was premeditated. On

November 17, 1899, Hilda Blake, after pleading guilty to murder, was sentenced to "hang by the neck until dead."

But the melodrama that surrounded Hilda's life did not end there. While jailed in Brandon, she kept the public's attention right up until the moment of her execution. She wrote poems that she had a friend send to the media for publication in which she alluded, though never actually stated, that some demon man had been responsible for her fall. She made a great display of singing ribald songs in prison then alternately turned weepy and coquettish. She used every trick she could to gain the sympathy of the people, particularly the men, who dealt with her. She never did, however, express any regret at what she had done.

One prominent visitor from Winnipeg was Dr. Amelia Yeomans, a leading voice of the Women's Christian Temperance Union. To support her organization's social reform campaign, Yeomans hoped to use Hilda as an example of an innocent young woman from a poor upbringing who was victimized by diabolical men. Yeomans was not surprised that Blake attempted to gain sympathy (and hopefully exoneration) for the murder; but she was appalled that the young woman admitted blatantly that she was guilty. Her diagnosis was that Blake was a "moral lunatic," a Victorian term used to describe someone who was mentally able to plan evil while having no moral inhibition against it. Yeomans felt that Blake was not only seriously morally damaged, but also dangerous. After her first encounter with Blake, Yeomans refused to meet with her again.

Hilda Blake was executed shortly after 8:30 AM on Wednesday, December 27, 1899, still behaving like the tragic heroine in one of her novels. Her last words: "Do not think too hardly of me. Good-bye."

CHAPTER FIVE

Nick Lysyk
Finagling Fraudster
(1950–)

On August 10, 2004, Nikolas Andrew Lysyk, former manager of a west Edmonton branch of the Bank of Montreal, was led away after being charged with defrauding his employer of close to $16 million. Lysyk's defence had been unique: severe depression brought on by his wife's infidelity. Upon sentencing, Lysyk broke down. He was facing seven years in prison and public humiliation brought on by his decision to steal money that didn't belong to him.

Nick Lysyk's life of crime began in 1996 when he started making fraudulent applications for bank loans at his branch. As branch manager, he had the authority to approve loans up to $50,000 without main branch approval—he used that authority to apply for loans for fictitious people, securing them with collateral that didn't exist. He secreted the money away right under the noses of his trusting employees by creating six accounts under false names. A routine auditor's check during August 2002 picked up an oddity: the signature on a loan to a Lillian Green was identical to the bank manager's. The auditor's check of the GIC used as collateral showed that the GIC did not exist.

An internal investigation followed which uncovered a total of 60 suspicious transactions managed by Lysyk. He was arrested on August 8, and two days later, charged with defrauding the bank of $16.3 million. He served six weeks in prison then was released on bail to await trial.

To date, only a small portion of the vast sum of money has been recovered through auction sales of confiscated property and personal effects. Lysyk admitted that the bank's money is gone, spent on property, a six-figure investment portfolio for his wife Jennifer and on gifts for a number of paid female escorts with whom he had developed relationships.

During Lysyk's trial, which took place in late August 2004, the court heard that various family members received payments ranging from $25,000 to $750,000. Seventeen properties, more than three dozen vehicles, high-end furniture and expensive jewellery were also purchased. With an annual salary in the $60,000 range, Lysyk must have come up with some very convincing stories to avoid suspicion over his suddenly enormous spending power.

Free on bail for the last two years, Lysyk has reconciled with his ex-wife. They lived together in downtown Edmonton until early September 2004, when Lysyk was arrested yet again for violating conditions of his bail. The charge of contacting one of his former girlfriends was dropped. On August 30, 2004, he pleaded guilty to defrauding the Bank of Montreal of $16.3 million, and on September 10, he was sentenced to seven years and four months in prison.

But Lysyk's troubles have only begun. He now faces a civil lawsuit launched by the Bank of Montreal. The bank hopes to recover as much as possible of the remaining $10 million of other people's money that Nick Lysyk stole and has not repaid.

CHAPTER SIX

John Schneeberger
Salacious Surgeon
(1961–)

It was November 16, 1996. Alice* was finally going to be believed. The man she had accused of the despicable crime of rape was her doctor, and he had already been free for too long. She was sure he had raped her, even though her memory of it had been altered. A private investigator managed to get a DNA sample from the doctor's car. It was a perfect match for the semen the rapist had left in her underclothing on that horrible night in the Kipling, Saskatchewan, hospital examination room nearly four years before when he injected her with a strong sedative and raped her. Now she finally had him. Or so she thought. John Schneeberger, adept at committing and then covering up his crimes by using his knowledge of medicine, was not about to be caught.

---

*Respecting a publication ban issued in November, 1999 (pursuant to section 486 sub 3 of the Criminal Code of Canada) preventing disclosure of the identity of the complainants or any information that could disclose their identities, no real names, other than the convicted man's, have been used in this chapter.

As the police made plans to collect another blood sample from the rapist doctor, Alice had reason to be nervous. Twice before, in November 1992, shortly after the rape, and again in August 1993, police had taken blood samples from Schneeberger. The DNA in the samples inexplicably did not match the DNA in the semen.

Publicly, Alice defied what seemed to be incontrovertible evidence of the doctor's innocence. She insisted to any and all who would listen that the 32-year-old doctor was guilty and that she would prove it. In return, the young woman, admittedly no angel, was hounded by townspeople in Kipling, Saskatchewan, the very town where she'd been raised. In a place where everyone knew your name and where gossip spread like butter on hot toast, Alice was an object of scorn and derision. She finally left Kipling when it was clear that few people believed her story.

Her parents, guilty of nothing other than standing behind their daughter, were also made to feel unwelcome in town. After Alice's allegations were made public, they received a letter from one of the only two medical clinics in town, the one in which Schneeberger practiced, indicating they would no longer be accepted there for treatment.

Alice knew she had to do something to bring an end to the life the whole horrible incident had forced her to lead, running from the place where she was comfortable. Once settled in another town miles away, she renewed her attempts to find out how it was that Schneeberger's blood sample had failed to match the DNA evidence of the semen.

The law firm representing Alice in her civil suit against Schneeberger contacted a retired RCMP officer with extensive background in undercover work and criminal investigation. He met with the young woman and, convinced of the truth of her story, agreed to investigate her story. He went through the reports of the investigation done by the Kipling detachment of the RCMP and immediately suspected that Schneeberger tampered with the evidence. His findings soon confirmed his suspicions. But for Alice, it had been a long and stress-filled wait.

❧

On October 31, 1992, Alice went to the Kipling Memorial Hospital asking to speak to a friend of hers who worked there. She was distraught from having had a terrible fight with her boyfriend and needed someone to talk to. As it turned out, the friend had already gone off duty. Alice, noticeably agitated, was asked by the night nurse if she wanted to be seen by the on-call doctor. Since her friend wasn't available, she thought talking to a doctor might ease her anxiety.

Alice was acquainted with Dr. Schneeberger, and she was happy to see him arrive at the hospital a few minutes after the nurse called him. Why wouldn't she be comfortable with him? After all, he was one of only two doctors in the community and had treated her on several other occasions.

Schneeberger escorted Alice into an examination room and spoke to her for a few minutes before suggesting a sedative might help her to calm down. Alice agreed, thinking he would prescribe pills. He returned moments later with a syringe, shutting the door behind him as he entered the room. Alice later reported that after being injected she had the sensation she could not move. She was aware of everything that was going on, but could not move her limbs or even speak. As her flaccid body slumped forward, the doctor caught her. He moved her to the examination table where he proceeded to rape her as she lay completely helpless—helpless, but sadly, not unaware of what was going on.

The doctor left, and a few minutes later, the nurse entered. Still groggy, Alice said nothing to the nurse about the assault. Feeling unable to drive home alone, Alice was permitted to stay at the hospital overnight. At noon the following day, Schneeberger returned to Alice's bedside. When he asked her how she was feeling, Alice wanted to know what kind of drug he had given her. He never answered her. She went home and made a decision that would change her life. She stuffed her panties into a plastic bag, determined to preserve the evidence of his assault and headed for Regina.

Assuming that a conflict between her word and that of the doctor would likely not go in her favour, she decided to have a rape test done in the much larger and more anonymous city of Regina, about 135 kilometres northwest of Kipling.

So, on November 1, 1992, Alice presented herself at a large hospital in Regina, filing a formal complaint of rape against Dr. John Schneeberger with the RCMP and with the Saskatchewan College of Physicians and Surgeons. As evidence, she produced the pair of panties she had been wearing the previous night.

A few days later, results of the test confirmed that Alice had been raped. Regina police contacted the local Kipling detachment. They, in turn, contacted Schneeberger to tell him of the charge and to ask him to voluntarily submit to DNA testing. Schneeberger quickly agreed to comply, making himself appear as a perfectly innocent man prepared to cooperate in every way he could. He wasn't innocent, but he was prepared.

In most small towns, gossip travels fast. Long before the police contacted the doctor, he was apprised of Alice's accusations. Aware that DNA evidence would convict him, he used his medical knowledge and the facilities available to him in the hospital to try to ensure that wouldn't happen.

In the privacy of his office, he injected his left arm with a local anaesthetic, then used antiseptic to scrub the area a few centimetres above his elbow. With a sharp scalpel, he made a narrow incision, and inserted a 15-centimetre tube, known to the medical community as a Penrose drain.

The Penrose drain is a small surgical device, usually made out of silicone, designed to promote drainage from surgical wounds. Since these catheters are pliable and sterile and therefore safe to be left under the skin for extended periods of time, Schneeberger knew the one he used was not going to fester. He also knew how to alter it to fit the unique use he intended for it. He filled it with blood collected earlier from a male patient in the hospital and sealed the straw-like device. With the tube of someone else's blood securely in place in his arm, Schneeberger was ready for his next move.

On the afternoon of November 16, 1992, a little over two weeks after Alice reported the rape in Regina, an RCMP officer met Schneeberger at the Kipling Hospital. Schneeberger acted the part of an innocent and cooperative, yet understandably resentful, citizen. He appeared for the blood test with the long sleeves of his sweater pulled down to cover his recent self-administered surgery. It appeared that the lab technician wasn't working quickly enough for the busy doctor. Muttering something about "doing it better myself," he grabbed the syringe from her, injected himself at the location where he knew the tube to be and handed the syringe back seconds later full of someone else's blood.

When the results of the first test came back negative, Alice insisted that it had to be a mistake, or worse, a conspiracy. She demanded a second DNA sample be taken. It was carried out in August 1993, with a surprise visit to Schneeberger's office by the Kipling RCMP detachment commander. As happened the first time, Schneeberger managed to insert the tube and take the sample himself. As before, the DNA sample did not match. The criminal case against him was dropped. The file remained open, but inactive.

Finally, three years later, Alice had the evidence that was going to convict her rapist. The private investigator working on her case had broken into Schneeberger's car and taken a DNA sample from a discarded stick of lip balm. Lab tests showed this DNA matched perfectly with the DNA of the semen sample from Alice's underwear from years before. This time she thought she had him. But Schneeberger was ahead of her again. The grapevine that had alerted the good doctor about Alice's first accusations alerted him that a private investigator was on his trail. He reinserted the vial of blood. The blood, although kept under refrigeration, was now some years older.

During the blood-sampling procedure, this time recorded on video, the lab technician commented that the blood didn't look fresh. Nevertheless, the sample was sent away to the lab, with the same startling result as before. But the police were certain Schneeberger was somehow tampering with evidence. They had since received a complaint from a second victim.

The second victim, only 13 at the time of the first incident, claimed Schneeberger had assaulted her after drugging her on at least two occasions. The years of the assaults were 1994 and 1995, the very same time that Alice was fighting a losing battle to convince police and the town that he was guilty. On evidence from the child's mother, police decided to get another DNA sample. This time, however, they did not take any chances. On December 16, 1997, with warrant in hand, they obtained several samples of the accused's DNA: hairs from Schneeberger's head, a blood sample taken from his fingertip by a lab technician, and a swab of skin cells from the inside of his cheek.

Several weeks later Schneeberger was charged with one count of sexual assault on Alice, two charges of administering a harmful substance, one charge of aggravated assault on the teenager and one charge of obstruction of justice.

Schneeberger pleaded not guilty to the charges of assault, indicating that the administration of the drugs was strictly for medical reasons. He admitted to the unconventional use of the Penrose drain, but claimed he had good reason for trying to fool police. A South African immigrant who came to Canada in 1987, he claimed that, as a boy, he had witnessed severe treatment by the police in his home country. He therefore did not trust the RCMP's ability to stand up for his rights, and he used the DNA ruse because he was afraid of being framed.

On November 25, 1999, the verdict was announced: guilty of drugging Alice and sexually assaulting her; guilty of sexually assaulting the teenager; guilty of obstructing justice. The Saskatchewan College of Physician and Surgeons immediately revoked his license to practice and struck his name from their register. Schneeberger was sentenced to a mere six years in prison, a verdict that shocked the victims and their families.

After losing two appeals, Schneeberger served the required two-thirds of his sentence. He was released on November 25, 2003. But his victims didn't have to worry that he would be back in their midst for very long.

In June 2004, in a twist that can only be called natural justice, Schneeberger was ordered deported to South Africa. It appears that while his trial was going on, Canadian officials found out that he had lied in his application for citizenship, which was granted in 1993. During the application interview, the citizenship judge asked him the standard question: "Are you under criminal investigation at this time?" His answer was "No."

Schneeberger, liar, rapist, ex-doctor and ex-convict, is now living in Durban, South Africa, with his mother.

CHAPTER SEVEN

❧❦❧

Edwin Alonzo Boyd
Gentleman Gangster
(1914–2002)

Toronto, Ontario, September 9, 1949

Thirty-five-year-old Ed Boyd dashed out of the Bank of Montreal on Avenue Road with a bag of cash that did not belong to him and became an overnight legend. He soon became known in the press by his full name, Edwin Alonzo Boyd. Plain old "Ed" just wasn't a glamorous enough handle for the fascinating crook who had captured the public's attention. In the late '40s and early '50s this charming and handsome young man with the Hollywood smile and the flashing eyes led his gang of bandits on a crime spree that included 11 Toronto-area bank hold-ups and two daring escapes from Toronto's Don Jail. It was neither insatiable greed nor destitution that led Boyd into a life of crime and to later become the subject of one of the nation's most massive manhunts. It was his desperate need to be successful at something.

Born on April 2, 1914, in Ontario's Muskoka region, Ed was the first-born child of Eleanor and Glover Boyd. Ed's early life seemed not so different from that of tens of thousands of other Canadian children whose fathers went off to war soon after they were born. Although his mother was neither well educated, nor particularly well informed about nutrition and child care, she treated Ed well, and they had a wonderful relationship.

There was however, terrible animosity between the boy and his father. Ed resented him when Glover came back after four years of overseas duty. Little Ed felt he had been replaced in his mother's affections. In the next few years, Eleanor and Glover had three more children, and moved frequently to accommodate the growing family. In 1921, Glover, an electrician by trade and a logger by experience, was accepted into the Toronto police department largely because of his overseas wartime service. The job of peace officer suited Glover well, for he was a deeply religious, authoritative man with a stern, military bearing. But the job did little to enhance his relationship with his eldest son Ed.

School held little interest for Ed, and he spent his time playing school sports or roaming around Toronto's downtown streets. At 14 years old, he was small, but he excelled at sports and was an amazing athlete. He was often seen by local people walking on his hands or doing back flips down the street. He played soccer and was a good skater and runner, but although he had the ability, his coaches felt he lacked the drive necessary to be a top-level competitor.

Ed's life took a sharp downward turn a few weeks before his 16th birthday, when his mother died of scarlet fever at age 48. Although Ed had begun working hard at school in order to qualify to learn a trade, his goal was never realized. Ed's father remarried soon after his wife died. He became so involved with his new wife, Minnie, that he reneged on his promise to send Ed to technical school. Glover signed Ed up to work on a relative's farm outside Toronto instead.

After two years, Ed decided to move back home, but he soon realized that his stepmother didn't want him there. In the summer of 1932, at the age of 18, Ed caught a freight train heading north, joining the flock of homeless and penniless men who rode the rails. It was in this milieu that Ed had his first run-ins with the law.

The Depression hit Canada hard, but its effects made themselves particularly felt in the West. With the western provinces technically bankrupt and their economies collapsed, jobs were scarce even for trained men; they were non-existent for an untrained youth with a grade eight education. A new-found friend Ed had met on the train between Toronto and Winnipeg taught him all he knew about panhandling. Ed found the new skill interesting, and he quickly mastered it.

After a brief but successful time in Winnipeg, he and his friend made their way to Edmonton where panhandling was not quite so well received. In November 1933, they were arrested for vagrancy and sentenced to six weeks in jail. Since he was carrying no identification of any kind, Ed passed himself off as John Wilson Harkaway, a fictional hero he had read about as a youngster.

After his release from jail, Ed returned home to Toronto for a while. Again, he felt he was unwelcome with his father's new wife. He went back to riding the rails, spending time in towns and cities along the way, always one step ahead of the police who continued to discourage panhandling. Just over a year after he was released from his first jail stint, Ed was arrested once more for vagrancy. This time, he spent two months in jail in Moosomin, Saskatchewan, and again, gave a name other than his own. Even though Edwin Alonzo Boyd had served two full terms in jail, he was still technically a man without a record. That soon changed.

In August 1936, after several months of panhandling, hitchhiking and freight hopping, Ed was again arrested for vagrancy. It was a short incarceration in Calgary—only three days—but it was an ominous sign of what came later. This time he was convicted as Edwin Alonzo Boyd.

Three weeks later Ed was arrested during a gas station break-and-enter in a small town just south of Saskatoon. He was sentenced to three years at the Saskatchewan Penitentiary in Prince Albert. Although Ed and his father had never achieved the kind of closeness that Ed enjoyed with his mother, Glover nevertheless used his influence as a respected police officer to win Ed early parole. In March 1939, Ed was released and sent home to Toronto where, with his father's influence, he got a job hoisting heavy milk cases at a local dairy. The physically demanding tasks encouraged Ed to keep in shape, and he began to focus his attention on physical fitness and nutrition. He walked the five kilometres to work and back each day and joined a local judo/karate club, quickly working his way up until he was instructing several classes a week in his off-hours. Ed liked the dairy job, and it paid well enough for him to buy himself a motorcycle. For a few months, things went well until one day his boss at the dairy reassigned him to the task of scrubbing out the enormous milk storage vats. Ed quit the dairy job, but he wasn't idle for long.

War was declared in the fall of that year. With his motorcycle license and martial arts skills under his belt (and a few lies on his application which claimed he had finished grade 10 and gone to technical school), Ed Boyd was recruited by the Royal Canadian Regiment. He trained as a dispatch rider and shipped out to England in December 1939. While serving in England, Ed met and married an Englishwoman, Dorreen Thompson, but Ed's life was once again marred by tragedy. Only two days after he was born, their first baby, a full-term healthy boy, was mortally injured during an air-raid evacuation. Fleeing the hospital, a nurse carrying several babies accidentally hit the Boyd baby's head against a doorframe. He died a few days later.

A letter Ed wrote to Dorreen at the time summed up the depth of his sorrow and gives a surprising glimpse into the heart of the man who was later referred to as Canada's Public Enemy Number One:

> ...*Your words tell me of your precious love for me and all the heartbreak of having our baby son snatched away. However, it was better that we hadn't a chance to get to know him....because it would have been harder that way....* (Lamb and Pearson, *The Boyd Gang*, p.16. Quoted from Vallée, 1997, p. 62)

Dorreen and Ed had three more children in England, and when the war was over, they moved back to Toronto, staying for a while with Ed's father and stepmother, then later moving into their own rented house at 44 Eglinton Avenue West. Shortly after Ed's official discharge, he was hired by the Toronto Transit Commission (TTC) as a shift-work streetcar conductor, his five and a half years of overseas military service a clear indication to them of the 31-year-old's skill and dependability. In their application screening, the TTC had discovered Ed's criminal record, but they decided the misspent youth was a result of the Depression rather than an inherent criminal nature.

Ed enjoyed his job with TTC, and the pay was sufficient for the Boyds to enjoy a reasonable lifestyle, but his wife wasn't satisfied. Dorreen began pressuring him to make more money and to get a job where he wouldn't have to do shift work. Ed finally quit in frustration. He worked for a short time at a few other jobs in the neighbour-hood—delivery truck driver, night watchman, bakery shop worker, even a brief attempt at setting up his own window-washing business, but nothing seemed to please him or to satisfy Dorreen. It was in late summer of 1949 that Ed Boyd read a piece in the newspaper which changed the path of his future.

Ed was looking through the paper to find a job offer that might interest him. His attention was caught by a short story about a mentally handi-capped teenager who had walked into a bank in Toronto and strolled out with $69,000. According to the write-up, the young man was appre-hended a few hours later, and the money was returned. The story did not have a glorious end-ing, but it inspired Ed Boyd.

His planned his first robbery well in advance. Boyd intended to make use of his athletic skill and his intelligence to ensure a safe and successful job. The only thing that was slightly below what he considered optimum level was his confidence as he sat in his car that September morning in

1949. He was glad he'd brought along some courage in a bottle of Irish whiskey.

He was going over the details of his plan before walking the few blocks to the Armour Heights Branch of the Bank of Montreal on Avenue Road, taking occasional glances into the rear view mirror at the face he had disguised with heavy make-up and cheek padding. As he sat, he sipped whiskey and fingered the Luger pistol he'd taken from the body of a dead German during the war. He was waiting for the "buzz" that told him the liquor was working.

After drinking more than half the bottle, he stepped out of the car and walked toward the bank. Unused to liquor, he was disturbed to find himself having trouble manoeuvring his way along the street. He almost abandoned the hold-up idea. Later he wished he had. The bank job did not go according to plan. His drunkenness made him slow and hesitant, and had it not been for good luck, Boyd would have been caught. He overstayed his time in the bank, failed to see two employees ring silent alarms, was almost shot by a bank employee, could not start his getaway vehicle and narrowly missed being stopped by police speeding towards the scene of the crime. As it was, he got away with just over $2000. He intended to do better the next time.

Planning for the next job began just after Christmas the same year when Boyd's money started to run out. He wanted to make sure he didn't make any mistakes this time, and he knew that superior organization was essential. More than four decades later, Boyd confided that he enjoyed the planning as much as the robberies themselves, and he was meticulous about it.

"I enjoyed planning a bank robbery," he told a reporter many years later. "Especially when I was doing it myself. Most important, it was knowing I could be successful."

He grew a moustache and rented several cheap storage garages in different locations, each under a different assumed name and each one padlocked. He began stealing cars, sometimes just for practice, returning them a short while later before the owner even knew they were gone. Other times he locked the stolen car away in one of his rented garages and left it there for later use. He took pains to learn the habits of the people working in the banks he targeted, and knew their schedules as well as they did. With far more confidence than he had for the first hold-up, he strolled, completely sober, into the Canadian Bank of Commerce on O'Connor Drive in Toronto just after noon on Wednesday, January 18, 1950, a time when he knew the building would be almost empty. He walked out with his white sugar bag full of cash.

The papers again splashed reports of the hold-up all over the front pages. This time the local story took precedence over the infamous Brinks Robbery, which had taken place the night before in Boston and had relieved Brinks of $1.5 million. Boyd's haul this time was $2862, only slightly more than the last. He consoled himself with the idea that he was getting better.

Ed Boyd had been able to keep the first heist a secret from Dorreen. The second wasn't so easy. When she confronted him about his elated mood and new-found riches, he admitted that he'd been robbing banks, and then with pride and excitement, filled her in on the details. Dorreen chose to stand by her man, and they spent the next few days literally laundering the money, putting the crisp new twenties through a soapless bath in the washing machine and drying them in the oven to make them look used. The money lasted about six months, and then it was time for Boyd to strike again. This time he wanted more.

His exhaustive research had taught him that he would never be able to pull off a major job alone, although he was aware of the inherent dangers of bringing in an accomplice. His first non-solo job on July 31, 1950, was with a partner named Howard Gault, a petty criminal. The hold-up went fairly smoothly but resulted in a meagre take of less than $2000 and a .38 revolver that Gault now carried. After divvying up the money, Boyd was left with less than he'd stolen from his solo jobs. He decided that having a partner wasn't worth it and went back to working alone. That decision turned out to be a mistake.

The next job on October 11, 1950, began well. Everything fell into place as Boyd had planned it, until the surprise appearance of an armed bank manager. The manager, seeing the hold-up, quickly grabbed his bank-issued pistol and fired three shots narrowly missing Boyd's head. Boyd fired two shots back, aiming high so he wouldn't hit the man. He then fled, this time empty-handed.

Boyd's realization that this was a near-disaster came later when he read the newspaper accounts. It was only then that he understood how close he had come to shooting someone...and to being shot. He knew he had to re-think his situation. He went back to legitimate work, this time on a street-repair crew side by side with his former partner, Gault. His hiatus from crime lasted less than three months.

By spring of 1951, Boyd was tired of the dirty and exhausting roadwork. He kept the job, but decided to do some unconventional moonlighting in his off-hours. He began planning another hold-up. The disguises had worked well, and he decided to continue using them. After his first hold-up at the Bank of Montreal, he had gone back without the disguise to see if anyone recognized him. No one had.

Whether out of curiosity or sheer perversity, Boyd decided to target that first bank again. Rather than use one of the cars he had stolen and stored, Boyd decided it was faster and less

complicated to simply steal a getaway car on the
way to the scene, like he'd done for the previous
two robberies.

Boyd's return engagement at the Armour Heights
branch of the Bank of Montreal in March 1951
went smoothly and in record time. In less than
two minutes, Boyd had lightened the bank's cof-
fers of just over $3000. It was his biggest take to
date, but it was still not enough.

Boyd knew he would get bigger hauls if he
started working with a partner again. He also had
one more reason to give up an honest living.
A minor accident occurred in July of that year.
Boyd received a shoulder injury when he was
struck by a truck while working on the road
gang, but he was refused workman's compensa-
tion. He decided he had no choice but to return
to crime.

Gault became his partner again along with
Boyd's younger brother Norm. In his senior
years, Boyd regretted the decision to lead his little brother into crime and admitted that Norm
had undoubtedly suffered greatly from the experience. But Norm's presence added to the efficiency of the plan, and on September 1, 1951,
the three made a hit at the Dominion Bank on
Lansing Street for a total take of $8029. Boyd had
the impression that things were looking up. They
weren't. Six weeks later, on a job Gault and Boyd
did without Norm, both were apprehended.

The foiled robbery on October 16, 1951 might have had a different outcome if it had not been for Boyd's over-confidence and Gault's drunkenness. As it was, the two men strutted into the bank at an hour when bank employees outnumbered customers by a ratio of about 10 to 1. One of the staff, overlooked by the robbers, pressed a silent alarm. While Boyd and Gault were rounding up the employees near the vault at the back, the police were already on their way. Gault was arrested on foot, minutes after running out of the bank and reluctantly handed over his revolver and the white sugar sack containing $12,234. Boyd was picked up in his stolen getaway truck a half-hour later. Boyd knew that Gault had been apprehended. That fact, along with the knowledge that the police had found his loaded gun and his makeup in the getaway vehicle, told Boyd the game was up. During questioning, he revealed that he had been responsible for this and the previous hold-ups. He was placed in the Don Jail to await sentencing and likely transfer to Kingston Penitentiary.

Don Jail was not the accommodation of choice in 1950s Toronto. The combination of tiny cells, Gothic architecture, menacing size and in-house gallows did nothing to make prisoners feel welcome. From the moment Edwin Alonzo Boyd was led into the building, he, like many guests before him, looked for a way to get out.

It didn't take him long to get to know some of his fellow inmates. Although he had remained anonymous during the first few robberies, his name and photo were now being plastered over the front pages of newspapers across the country. Within a few days of being jailed, Boyd became a star. His notoriety impressed two men whose cells were near his own: Lennie Jackson, an armed robber with underworld connections, and Willie Jackson (no relation to Lennie), a one-legged violent mugger and armed robber. They had read of his exploits in the newspapers and were quick to make nice with Boyd. They were just as quick to make plans.

On November 4, they climbed down a ladder made of bed sheets after sawing their way through window bars. They used a hacksaw that Lennie Jackson had hidden in his wooden leg. Once free, the trio hightailed it to a predetermined location, a rooming house in Toronto owned by the parents of Steve Suchan, a trigger-happy criminal who was dating Lennie's sister. The group managed to stay out of trouble for all of two weeks. On November 20, 1951, four men led by a lean, wiry and athletic Edwin Alonzo Boyd, burst into the Bank of Toronto on Dundas and Bousted, and made off with $4300. Ten days later, the same four men held up the Royal Bank on Leaside and went home with $46,000. The Boyd Gang was born.

Many more bank hold-ups were attributed to the Boyd Gang over that winter, but their guilt was only proven in three. Bank robbery was somewhat trendy among a certain segment of Toronto's population, but none of the many bank robbers received the press coverage that the Boyd Gang did. Reporters seemed ready to publish every tidbit of information they could get about them, and what they couldn't gather, they embellished or made up.

Meanwhile, Boyd's money was dwindling fast. A wanted man, Boyd was at the same time try-ing to do best by his family. Odd as it may seem, while the infamous Edwin Alonzo Boyd was being turned into a dashing folk hero by the competitive Toronto media, he was working hard to support his wife, a 10-year-old son and 8-year-old twins, a boy and a girl. He was quoted later, recalling that time: "It was kind of difficult to be a member of a bunch of crooks and at the same time to raise a family. I tried to do it but it wasn't possible."

Boyd's shady business continued. Although he had different accomplices at each hold-up, Edwin Alonzo Boyd was a constant presence, always reported by eyewitnesses as handsome, athletic, calm, confident, organized, and gentlemanly. They seemed quite happy to overlook the fact that he was also stealing their money.

Unfortunately, both of the Jacksons turned out to be weak links for the Boyd Gang. A week before

Christmas 1951, Willie Jackson, who was hiding out in Montreal with Lennie and Steve Suchan, did something Boyd had always warned against—drawing attention to himself. Jackson was in a bar, flaunting the fat roll of money he carried, and waving his gun around in the men's washroom to show how tough he was. One customer clearly was not impressed. He called the police. Willie was sent up for an extended stay at Kingston Penitentiary.

In the meantime, Mary Mitchell, Lennie Jackson's sister and Steve Suchan's girlfriend, was getting up to no good of her own. She discovered that Steve had been seeing another woman, who was about to give birth to his baby. She began to have regular meetings with the police, offering bits of information that helped them to keep track of the gang's activities. Even more damaging, she began telling lies about Boyd to Suchan and Lennie Jackson, claiming that Boyd had beaten her and burned her. The gang was beginning to come apart.

Christmas must have been hard on the gang's pocketbooks. A January 25, 1952 hold-up of the Bank of Toronto, with Suchan and a new member of the gang, Willie Jackson's brother Joe, netted $10,400. It was enough to keep them happy for a time. Then, on March 4, Joe Jackson went along with Boyd on what would be the last hold-up committed by the notorious Boyd Gang for a while. The heist itself, $24,696, was certainly not their most successful financially, but it did solidify Edwin Alonzo Boyd's cult hero status. The press coverage the next day varied somewhat, but all of it had the same tone: Edwin Alonzo Boyd was larger than life. As one smitten female bank-teller recalled, "...I couldn't do anything but stare. I just couldn't turn away from the calm one...the leader. I was fascinated by him."

Two days after the March 4 hold-up, two police detectives following up on a tip from Mary, stopped a car containing Suchan and Lennie Jackson. In the scuffle that followed, Steve Suchan shot and mortally wounded Detective Edward Tong.

As Tong lay in hospital fighting for his life, attitudes toward the Boyd Gang turned against them. The married 26-year-old father of two young children, Tong was one of the most popular and effective police officers in the city of Toronto. Cops loved him; the public loved him. Even criminals had to admit to a grudging respect and admiration for him. He was brave, upright and never gave away a source. When he finally succumbed to his wounds a few days later, the members of the Boyd Gang were no longer heroes.

Suchan was arrested within hours of Tong's shooting. Lennie was apprehended one week later. The shooting put renewed interest into the recapture of Boyd, considered to be the kingpin of the gang's activities. He was arrested at home in bed and without a struggle, in the early morning hours of March 15, 1952. With Willie and Joe Jackson already serving time, the Boyd Gang was now safely behind bars. But not for long.

Whether out of compassion for the criminals or a smug belief that the gang would never try another jailbreak, the authorities housed the four men they had just captured in the same cellblock. Suchan, Boyd and the two Jacksons ate together, exercised together and played cards together. Together, they also planned another escape.

On the morning of September 8, 1952, while their lawyers were busy gathering ammunition for the upcoming trials, the four members of the Boyd Gang were busy letting themselves out of the Don Jail for the second time. They unlocked one cell with a key Willie had fashioned, pushed out some previously filed-down bars and went over the jail's outside wall.

A massive manhunt was waged; the reward was $26,000. Police forces on both sides of the Quebec-Ontario border were eager to put the gang behind bars. It seemed the public was too. On September 16, 1952, on a tip from a local farmer, the four escapees were surrounded in the barn where they were hiding. The Boyd Gang had had its last taste of freedom.

At trials that took place over the next few weeks, punishments were meted out in proportion to the crimes committed: Willie Jackson was given 29 years. Suchan and Lennie Jackson were sentenced to death for the murder of Detective Tong. They were hanged on December 16.

The trial of Edwin Alonzo Boyd, beginning on September 22, occupied a great deal of the public's and the media's attention. Testimony showed that Boyd was neither as dangerous nor as ruthless as he had been made out to be. During the trial, even the police who pursued and finally apprehended him, testified under oath that Boyd never intentionally hurt anyone, and despite many opportunities to shoot at or injure police and bystanders, never did. The judge remained unimpressed. Boyd's sentence went on for several paragraphs: eight life terms for the bank robberies, plus 32 more years for related offences that included auto theft and jailbreak. Terms were concurrent, meaning that with good behaviour, he might have a hope of early release. Refusing to take advantage of his notoriety to gain favour with the guards or special treatment from other prisoners, Boyd became a model prisoner, getting group counselling and impressing prison authorities with his insights into his own behaviour. As a result of his exemplary behaviour, he earned several hundred days of remission from his sentence. Considered no threat to reoffend, he was released on parole for the last time on October 30, 1966. He was 52.

Edwin Alonzo Boyd had gone from celebrity to undesirable in just a few months. During their crime spree, the Boyd Gang collectively stole slightly more than $100,000, yet their antics, real and imagined, had been the central focus for the citizens of Toronto far longer than any other single topic.

By the time Boyd was released from prison, he was divorced from his wife and the public had almost forgotten him. He made the transition to civilian life by moving to BC and legally changing his name. He spent the rest of his life caring for his second wife, a disabled woman he met while driving a bus for the handicapped. He died quietly in 2002 after sharing with the public deep regret about his life and how differently from his intentions it had turned out.

CHAPTER EIGHT

Klaus Burlakow
Bureaucrat Bandit
(1954–)

A rose by any other name would smell as sweet, wrote William Shakespeare. Klaus Burlakow likely doesn't agree. In fact, if Klaus Burlakow is to be believed, his name turned him into a bank robber. The Winnipeg man's problems started in 2002 when he decided to rob banks to support his out-of-control spending habits. And oh, what a tangled web he wove...

The son of Russian immigrants, Burlakow grew up in the North Kildonan district of Winnipeg, a largely working-class area of town mostly populated by Mennonites and Polish and Ukrainian immigrants. His parents were hard-working, but his upbringing was not without its drama. His father, a steelworker and reportedly a heavy drinker, shot and wounded a neighbour who was stealing from him. Otherwise, Klaus had an early life that was not much different from those of his friends. He graduated from

Daniel McIntyre Collegiate in 1972 and received a Bachelor of Arts degree at the University of Winnipeg.

During university and after graduation, he worked at a variety of jobs, mostly with Winnipeg's Department of City Parks and Recreation. In 1997, when he had been married for many years to his high school sweetheart Brenda, with whom he had two teenage children, Burlakow landed a plum job. He was hired as an event planner for the City of Winnipeg at a salary of over $120,000 a year.

Although marketing courses taken at the University of Manitoba and management courses from Red River College no doubt gave him the paper suitability for the senior administrative position, it was more likely his outgoing personality was what clinched it for him. He worked at the job for four years, skilfully organizing such major events as the Canadian Figure Skating Championships in 2001, the 1999 Pan American Games and countless other high-profile occasions. Throughout his term in the Mayor's office, Burlakow had his supporters and his detractors. Supporters claimed he was a tremendous organizer: someone who could get the job done regardless of obstacles. Detractors saw Burlakow as an aggressive bully: an abrasive, arrogant loudmouth who thought he was smarter than everyone else.

Burlakow's neighbours in North Kildonan mostly avoided him, aware of him as a loud and blustery showoff. Given to driving like a madman through the neighbourhood, he was warned more than once to slow down for the sake of the children.

Burlakow's style was not appreciated in the new tone of courtesy and gentility that pervaded after Mayor Glen Murray took office in 1998. Murray's staff, accustomed to more gentlemanly dealings, did not tolerate Burlakow's pushy ways for long. Late in 2001, Burlakow was encouraged to take an early retirement package, which included a generous severance payment of close to $170,000.

Despite over four years of salaries in the top percentages of the Canadian population, Burlakow was in financial trouble. Years of bad investments coupled with injudicious spending had landed the family in severe debt. Money borrowed from friends and Burlakow's elderly and recently widowed mother helped, but not enough. With his high-paying job gone, Klaus Burlakow needed some other way to support his spending habits. A few months after his departure from the Mayor's office, he decided to get into a new kind of event planning—armed bank robbery.

On November 6, 2002, his attempt to rob a bank was unsuccessful. Dressed like a robber from a B-rated film in a black jacket, black pants and black knit watch cap pulled low over his forehead, Burlakow entered the Scotiabank at 1220 Pembina Highway in Winnipeg. He shoved a note through the wicket and waved his air pistol around. The quick-thinking bank teller slipped a dye pack into a bundle of bills before handing it over. The armed, heavy-set robber didn't get far before the packet of red dye burst, covering his clothes and the cash. Dropping the money and his gun, and leaving most of his outer clothing behind, he fled the scene in his waiting black Ford Expedition.

His next heist was in January 2003. This time Burlakow targeted the Scotiabank at the Pacific Centre Mall in Vancouver, and this time his project was more successful. He made off with almost $3000. Back in Winnipeg on January 21, 2003, Burlakow robbed the CIBC on Roblin Boulevard and went home $2000 richer. Three days later, he robbed a Scotiabank in the St. James area of Winnipeg. The haul was nearly $5000. Over the next three weeks, several more banks in Winnipeg were hit, with takes averaging $2000 to $3000. But Valentine's Day 2003 was to be the day of Burlakow's undoing.

It did not take much for police to outthink a criminal who usually hit the same banking establishments (Scotiabanks) in the same end of the city (southwest), using the same method, disguise and vehicle. Burlakow's trick of slapping stolen license plates on his vehicle did not throw police off his trail as much as he counted on.

On the afternoon of February 14, Burlakow robbed the Scotiabank at 528 Waterloo Street, and the police were ready for him. As he pulled out of his parking spot with the stolen bait money tucked into his shirt and his air pistol in one hand, a police cruiser pulled in behind him with lights flashing and siren wailing. Burlakow didn't stop. He led police on a highspeed chase through busy residential streets, and often hit speeds in excess of 150 kilometres per hour as he raced toward the outskirts of town. By the time he reached the Trans-Canada bypass west of the city, he was clocked at over 160 kilometres per hour. With police in hot pursuit, Burlakow, travelling at breakneck speed, lost control of his vehicle. The big SUV skidded off Hwy. 2 near Starbuck, Manitoba. Burlakow was unable to regain control as it ploughed through the heavy snow before it became wedged in a deep drift and stopped. Officers approached cautiously with firearms drawn and ordered Burlakow to throw out his weapon. Burlakow tossed the air pistol out onto the snow, and officers pulled his bulk, more than 160 kilos of it, through the window of his vehicle.

With his arrest, Burlakow's 15 minutes of fame multiplied. When his identity was revealed, he was instantly dubbed the bureaucrat bandit by the media. Then, only days after the fugitive's arrest, Cathy Taylor, a married woman in Seattle, contacted Winnipeg police. She told them that Burlakow had engaged in even more exciting adventures south of the border. Taylor, a frequent internet surfer, had recognized Burlakow's photo from online news reports. But this armed bank robber from Winnipeg seemed to have nothing, other than a face, in common with the man she knew as Patrick Burke.

Cathy Taylor said they had met on an internet chat line late in 2001. The two developed what was purported to be a business relationship after the man travelled to Seattle several times to meet with her. Burlakow, calling himself Burke, passed himself off as an Irish millionaire, brogue and all. Staying in Seattle's finest hotels, paying for dinners at the pricey Sorrento Hotel, wearing high-end clothing and driving rented luxury cars, it wasn't long before Burlakow convinced Taylor that he would be an excellent business partner with financial resources to spare.

It seems Taylor and the hefty would-be Irishman shared a dream to organize major events, both corporate and public, on the West Coast. The two travelled together, sometimes to check out potential venues, sometimes just to enjoy each other's company or the company of Taylor's husband and family. To Taylor's later distress, in January 2003, Burlakow had her drop him off at a location in Vancouver so he could attend a meeting. Little did Taylor know that Burlakow's meeting was with a frightened bank teller looking down his pistol at the Pacific Centre Mall's Scotiabank.

While Taylor contemplated an exciting and lucrative business future, Burlakow plied her with sympathy-evoking lies about his past life in Ireland. He claimed he was raised in strife-torn Belfast, saw his first wife blown up in an IRA-related car bombing, was recruited by the IRA because of his superior intellect and was going through a nasty divorce with his current wife, a greedy Nova Scotia woman named Brenda. Burlakow was so intent on creating the fictional person named Patrick Burke that he even involved his son, who posed as 16-year-old Michael Burke on one of his visits to Taylor in Seattle.

But the story Burlakow wove for Taylor was only a prelude to the whoppers he told police after a few months of inspirational seclusion in Stoney Mountain Penitentiary. According to the new story, facing discrimination in Winnipeg, Burlakow wanted desperately to get out of that city and make his real mark on the world. It was his new business partners in Vancouver who drove him to bank robbing.

Burlakow said he was a victim of discrimination because of his name. He was unable to get ahead in WASP Winnipeg, where he was undervalued because of his ethnicity. People treated him like a bumpkin, not because of his behaviour but because of his unpronounceable name.

In the early part of 2002, after his retirement from the Mayor's office, he set up an events promotion company in the city he despised. Soon realizing he couldn't make a go of it there, he set his sights on Vancouver.

Burlakow allegedly contacted investors through someone he knew in Winnipeg. Burlakow claims he knew the investors were not squeaky clean, but he consoled himself that he was not really a crook, just someone doing what was necessary to make a living.

According to Burlakow, his investors insisted he start living the high life, even though he couldn't afford it. Eventually, the beleaguered Burlakow, desperately trying to keep up with his hoodlum business partners, borrowed money from his mother. According to the supposedly reluctant criminal, that was not the end of it.

The phantom investors next forced Burlakow to become involved in shady money laundering fronted by musical events and then later into cross-border drug-smuggling. The venture went up in smoke when one of the investors ran off with most of the investment money and the others got cold feet. They demanded an immediate return of their $50,000 investment or they would hurt Burlakow's family. And that, according to Klaus Burlakow, was why he robbed banks.

Later, the threats against his family were mysteriously withdrawn, as was the requirement that he repay his debt to the investors. Burlakow has never revealed the names of any of his associates and no evidence has come to light to substantiate any of his claims. With preposterous tales like this under his belt, it isn't at all surprising that Burlakow's favourite prison pastime is writing fantasy fiction for children.

He was ordered to repay over $25,000 to the banks he robbed, and sentenced to eight years in prison. He is currently serving time at Manitoba's Stoney Mountain Penitentiary. He may be eligible for parole some time in 2005, if he can come up with a story good enough to convince the parole board.

CHAPTER NINE

Valentine Shortis
Aristocratic Assassin
(1875–1941)

In the quiet last hours of 1895, as the rest of Montréal waited for the clock to strike midnight and the calendar to turn over another year, a handsome young man sat in his death row prison cell calmly sipping tea and eating shortcake. Scheduled to hang in just three more days, Valentine Shortis gave every impression of being unconcerned about the fate that awaited him. As it turned out, he might have known something few other people knew—that the hanging would not take place.

On the night of March 1, 1895, shortly after 10:00 PM, Valentine Shortis strolled into the payroll office of the Montréal Cotton Company where he had recently been employed. Shortis seemed his usual eccentric, nonchalant self. He eased himself into a chair and, while he ate an apple, chatted with four colleagues who were filling pay envelopes.

Shortis casually began talking to John Lowe, the payroll manager, about the loaded revolver they all knew was kept in a desk drawer. He asked Lowe if he could look at it. Lowe ignored the request and went back to the pay envelopes.

A few minutes later, Shortis, a known gun collector, made the request again, this time claiming to be interested in checking the gun's serial number. Lowe went to the drawer and removed the gun, emptying it of bullets before handing it over. Shortis made a great display of examining the gun, praising its quality and polishing it before handing it back to Lowe with a nod. Lowe reloaded the gun and replaced it in the drawer.

The men continued to sit and chat, laughing over a joke one of them made about the ongoing battle over the use of French and English languages in Manitoba schools.

"Manitoba's lawmakers ought to come to Québec," said Arthur Leboeuf. "They would see how French and English can work together, hein?" He poked one of the other men in the ribs as he said this, bringing more laughter to the room.

Hugh Wilson was just opening the large walk-in vault. He turned to respond, but the words did not pass his lips. Shortis lunged for the gun and fired point-blank into Wilson's chest. One of the other men, John Loy, scrambled to his feet and ran towards the telephone. Shortis shot him in the head at close range, killing him instantly.

Paymaster Lowe and Arthur Leboeuf grabbed as much money as they could and raced into the vault, pulling the door closed after them and holding it against Shortis' attempts to pull it open. Shortis called through the closed vault door for Lowe and Leboeuf to come out and help him with the dying Hugh Wilson. A quick-thinking Lowe shouted back that the vault door was stuck. He told Shortis to turn the dial on the door. Shortis did as he was told, effectively locking Lowe and Leboeuf safely away from him and his loaded gun.

An angered Shortis turned to see a trail of blood on the floor leading away from the spot where Wilson, his first victim, had fallen. He traced the bloody path out into the factory, striking matches to light his way though the dark and near-deserted building. When he found Wilson some distance away, he shot him again and left him for dead. But the carnage wasn't over.

Shortis carried the matches back to the payroll office and lit a fire of trash in front of the locked vault, intending to smoke out Lowe and Leboeuf. Maxime Leboeuf, the night watchman and brother of the Leboeuf man in the vault, smelled the smoke and came to investigate. As the watchman opened the office door, Shortis took aim and fired. Leboeuf was dead before he hit the floor.

Meanwhile, Wilson, who survived one bullet wound to the chest and a second to the neck, crawled to the furnace room to warn the worker on night duty. The worker called police and a doctor and then charged to the payroll office armed with an iron bar. Shortis immediately surrendered the gun and threw his hands in the air. When the police arrived, Shortis was tied to a chair. He said calmly, "I'm the man. Shoot me."

Shortis was escorted without protest to the police station and charged with two murders. During the lengthy trial that followed, it was revealed that, although Shortis was barely 20, he had quite a string of aggressive incidents in his background.

Francis Valentine Cuthbert Shortis, called Valentine in honour of his February 14 birthday, belonged to a wealthy Irish family. He was an only child and a singularly spoiled one, with all the privileges his parents, particularly his mother, could lavish on him. At the age of 16, his father, supposedly to teach him independence, sent him on his own to Montréal, where the family had business connections.

Valentine went to work as a secretary at the Montréal Cotton Works which was housed outside the city in the nearby village of Victoriaville, a locale that much later became known as the producer of world-famous hockey sticks. Valentine's job did not work out as well as planned, and it was arranged that the secretarial job would be given to someone more qualified. Young Valentine was kept on without pay in order to learn the business.

As soon as they heard about the shootings, Valentine's parents travelled to be at his side. They quickly used their considerable connections to hire what many considered to be the best defence team in the nation: Henri St. Pierre, George Foster, and J.N. Greenshields, who had been one of Louis Riel's defence attorneys 10 years earlier. The crack team travelled to Ireland and assembled the largest contingent ever brought into Canada at one time to act as character witnesses. What was unusual about the testimony of the witnesses was that it made the accused look worse than he had before the trial. This was no accident. The defence team was aiming for an acquittal based on the contention that Valentine Shortis was not capable of reasoning the wrongness of his actions, and therefore was not responsible for the horrific crime. They were going for a plea of insanity.

The stories from witnesses were numerous and became more and more convincing as the trial went on. Many stories indicated that young Valentine was extremely cruel to animals. He was seen stabbing one of his father's dogs while laughing uproariously. He once stuck a pitchfork into several of his father's cows, then stood laughing as they writhed about in agony. Once he tethered a cat, then shot at it to see how many bullets it could take before it finally fell to the ground.

An accomplished rider, young Valentine seemed to have enjoyed some rather unorthodox sport from horseback, such as galloping down railway tracks in front of speeding trains or cantering through the streets of Waterford with a stick in his hand, beating about the head anyone who didn't get out of his way. He once rode a horse through the town's butcher shop. On another occasion he rode his pony over an older child who teased him in an attempt to trample him.

Although not unusually scholarly, Valentine did make a mark at school with his playful and mischievous manner. In fact, his former head-master at the Christian Brothers School in Waterford remembered him as a childish, eccentric and vain child who suffered quite regularly from terrible headaches. During these headaches, his behaviour was sometimes uncontrollable and bizarre.

There were also incidents that suggested that Valentine Shortis had as little regard for people as he had for animals. He once fired his pistol at a young girl, grazing her arm. He was so amused by the resulting chaos that he applauded himself loudly as she was being taken away for medical attention. One time, he fired his revolver into the crowd during a day at the races. No one was hurt, but he certainly caused quite a stir. While on a train on his way to a county fair, he once set fire to a newspaper as a gentleman sharing his compartment was reading it. Returning home, he lit gunpowder under one of the seats and nearly set the whole train car on fire.

Bizarre as these incidents were, no one saw fit at the time to tell his parents. Mr. and Mrs. Shortis appeared dumbfounded when the witnesses, one after another, told these tales about the horrific deeds of their sweet-faced young son. When asked why the parents were never told, several witnesses admitted they had not wanted to burden the well-liked and admired parents. Others suggested that they didn't want to insult or trouble the parents. Still, others intimated that they didn't want to become known as informers in the tightly knit community.

As the trial progressed, it was clear his defence team had made a clever decision to prove Valentine insane and thus get him off the charges.

According to testimony, Valentine's recent behaviour also showed a major lack of restraint and maturity. Valentine, after his arrival in the Montréal area, had quickly developed a reputation as an annoying young man. While living in an apartment on Commissioner Street, he was asked by the custodian to leave because tenants had complained of his behaviour. They complained that he regularly thundered up and down the stairs two or three at a time, shaking the whole building. The tall, handsome and playful Valentine had flirted with the custodians' wife, throwing kisses to her as he passed their ground floor apartment. This, perhaps more than the tenants' complaints, may have been the real reason for his eviction.

There were other behaviours reported at the trial that lent credence to his being labelled as a fool or a madman. He reportedly often ate his meals from the bottom up, ordering dessert first, then ending with soup, with the main course tucked in between. His taste in clothes was, at the very least, peculiar. He often sported a bright red sash around his waist and showed up at one Black Tie affair wearing buckskin moccasins and a rope holding up his trousers. He regularly went barefoot in his building and was once observed washing his sock-clad feet in the basin of a public washroom. When finished, he removed the wet socks, stuffed them into his pocket and put the boots on over his wet bare feet. He was also known to spit on people in public, for no apparent reason.

Many of these incidents would bring nothing more than a glance today. But in staid, conformist upper class Victorian Montréal, such behaviour was viewed as outrageous or bizarre, and was identified as the product of a diseased mind. The defence was going precisely the way his attorneys hoped it would.

Lawyers for the prosecution made valiant efforts to show aspects of Valentine's behaviour that indicated level-headedness and lucidity, but unfortunately, there was a shortage of convincing illustrations.

Defence lawyers smugly countered with evidence based on another widely accepted view.

They showed there was a family history of insanity. It was another score for the defence.

In the 1890s, psychiatrists were arguing strongly that heredity was a major factor in mental illness. A number of Valentine's relatives had died in the Clonmel Lunatic Asylum in Ireland including Valentine's grandfather. He died in 1891 at the age of 65 of "softening of the brain", a disease which manifested itself in hallucinations and was likely what we know today as Alzheimer's. An uncle was 39 when he died of epilepsy and disease of the spine. The uncle's history included several admissions to the asylum for uncontrollable violence.

Valentine's mother's family was not without its mental problems. Among the members of her immediate family who had also been in the asylum were her sister, an uncle, and a nephew. The prosecution's chances of forcing Valentine Shortis to take responsibility for his crime were looking more and more grim.

Not wishing to leave anything to chance, the defence team came up with a third strike supporting the plea of insanity. They found statistics indicating that the proportion of people in insane asylums who had tuberculosis was double the proportion in the general population. An erroneous leap of logic was made, and generally accepted at the time, that people with tuberculosis were more likely to be insane than those who did not have the disease. The judge reminded the defence attorneys to show what possible relevance these findings had to the proceedings. The spectators in court were already anticipating his answer—Valentine Shortis had symptoms that showed he likely suffered from tuberculosis, or consumption as it was then called. With behaviour, heredity and now consumption all linking Valentine Shortis to mental instability, a verdict of not guilty by reason of insanity seemed to be a foregone conclusion.

But neither the defence manoeuvrings nor the eyewitness reports of Valentine's unorthodox behaviour were enough to block from the 12-man jury's memory the terrible deeds which had been visited on the innocent and well-known men who were either already dead, or had fought for their lives. After 29 record-setting days in session, court was adjourned. A verdict was reached.

On that beautiful, clear November 3 morning, elegantly attired in a black suit and tie, his blond hair brushed neatly, Valentine Shortis was found guilty of first-degree murder. The following day he appeared again in the same court and awaited sentencing with the same vacant, preoccupied expression that had been on his face throughout the trial. Mr. Justice Michel Mathieu slowly donned the customary black cap. His voice choking with emotion, he sentenced Valentine Shortis to death by hanging. The prisoner, calmly and showing no signs of anxiety, thanked the judge and obediently accompanied the guards to Beauharnois Prison in Montréal to await execution on January 3.

Within hours of sentencing, Mr. and Mrs. Shortis and defence counsel submitted a bid for clemency to the Governor-General-in-Council. From that point on, a steady cast of highly placed individuals from both sides of the Atlantic became involved, including Governor General Lord Aberdee, his wife Lady Ishbel Aberdeen and the federal minister of justice, Charles Hibbert Tupper. Even the prime minister himself, Mackenzie Bowell, was involved. Petitions, personal communications, and even private visits were undertaken by the Shortis parents and their many influential friends and supporters, but a decision to commute the sentence continued to be delayed.

On December 31, 1895, J.R. Radclive, the official Canadian hangman, travelled from his home in Toronto to Beauharnois Prison to supervise the construction of the gallows and to orchestrate arrangements for all required communications to the public. A black flag was to be hoisted from a prominent location on the prison at the moment of execution. Local church bells were to be rung for 15 minutes as the execution was carried out. Radclive was also asked to arrange for Valentine's body to be delivered intact to his mother for burial. The scene was grim. But not, apparently, in Valentine's cell.

Valentine Shortis spent what were expected to be his last days on earth taking great pains with his appearance, planning gourmet meals for himself and having tea parties during his mother's daily visits. To many who viewed him, Valentine reacted to death row as if he was on a holiday, reading, chatting and singing. On December 31, Valentine Shortis calmly went to bed believing that it would be his last New Year's Eve alive.

On New Year's Day morning, officials at the prison received a letter from Lord Aberdeen informing them that the 12 members of his council were still tied in their decision, even after four meetings in session. Governor General Lord Aberdeen, in his position, was charged with the duty of breaking the tie vote. He decided to commute the death sentence to life imprisonment. The prisoner was to be moved immediately to St. Vincent de Paul Penitentiary to be incarcerated as a criminal lunatic for the rest of his natural life.

The story does not end there. After 41 years in various prisons throughout Québec and Ontario, Valentine Shortis was released on April 3, 1937 at the age of 62. He began his new life as Francis Cuthbert, and giving his age as 40, fulfilled a long-held dream of joining the army. The army knew his true identity, and that the conditions of his release disallowed him from leaving Canada, so he was allowed to serve and train with the Queen's Own Rifles home unit. He was able to join his regiment in the march past when King George VI and Queen Elizabeth, the mother of our present queen, visited Toronto in 1939. This was an ironic situation for a man once charged with multiple murders.

One bit of information about him, believed by many of the well-connected people who sought his release, was never revealed during the trial. They believed that Valentine Shortis' father was an illegitimate son of Prince Albert. If this was true, it made Valentine Shortis a member of the royal family. It may explain the number of high-status individuals who lobbied, first for his pardon, and throughout the years of his imprisonment, for his parole.

Valentine Shortis died on April 30, 1941, of a heart attack, shortly after complaining of feeling ill. No one claimed the body, and his remains are buried in an unmarked grave in Toronto's Mount Hope Cemetery.

CHAPTER TEN

Léo Bertrand
Dastardly Doctor
(1913–1953)

Léo Bertrand, nattily dressed and characteristically aloof, returned to his apartment in Ottawa to make plans for his future. In two years, the 22-year-old Bertrand went from life as a single man living with his parents in a small Québec village, to the accused murderer of his pregnant wife, to a free man who was awarded a $10,000 life insurance policy. However, his freedom lasted no longer than the money. Adopting the name The Tuxedo Kid, he was a man destined for trouble.

Léo Bertrand grew up on the farm near Ste. Justine-de-Newton in western Québec where he was born on July 13, 1913. Like many rural children from big families, Léo and his siblings did not receive the benefit of any education beyond grade school. Léo worked on the family farm until he met and married Rose Marie Asselin, a pretty young girl from a neighbouring village.

The couple moved to Ottawa where Léo found a job as a taxi driver, and by the time Rose became pregnant a short while later, they had savings enough to afford a small apartment. One of the friends they made in their new neighbourhood was an insurance man by the name of Eugene Picard. Picard was a seasoned salesman of the relatively new thing called life insurance, and the idea quickly appealed to Bertrand's vanity and greed. After giving a brief explanation of the policy and a thorough explanation of the double-indemnity clause, Picard was happy to be able to write up a policy.

Bertrand, for his part, was surprised that any company would pay him $5000 if his healthy young wife should die. He was absolutely shocked to find out they would pay him double that if the death was accidental. Before the ink on the contract was dry, Bertrand was planning how he would spend the money.

On December 19, 1934, Bertrand received his signed copy of the insurance certificate with the glossy red notarized seal and his name in large bold letters next to the word "beneficiary." The following day, Bertrand booked off sick from his taxi job and, together with his pregnant young wife, took a drive on the pretty snow-packed country roads of Beauharnois-Salaberry County.

They stopped for a pleasant visit with Rose's parents in their small community just across the Québec-Ontario border not far from Valleyfield.

They shared a delicious homecooked meal and set off shortly after dark to return to Ottawa. It was the last time Rose's parents saw their daughter alive.

After leaving the farmhouse, Léo announced they would take a scenic route home. It was a lovely moonlit night, so it seemed a good idea. As they approached the village of St. Polycarpe, Rose was surprised when Léo made an abrupt turn that faced them toward the lake instead of toward the highway.

"I think it's a little too cold for a swim," she chuckled. "Don't you think we should be heading for home?"

Léo didn't answer. His gloved hands gripped the steering wheel, and he stared straight ahead, seemingly intent on his driving.

"Léo?" Rose prompted.

Still no answer. Suddenly Léo put his foot to the floor. The car sped through a stop sign, barely missing a pedestrian crossing the intersection.

"Please slow down," Rose said. "You are frightening me."

Léo sped along St. Polycarpe Road and brought his car to a sudden stop on the pier at the end of the road.

Minutes later, Léo was pounding on the door of a nearby house.

"My car is in the lake," Léo shouted, waving his arms frantically. "It went off the end of the pier. My wife...she is inside!"

Léo and the house's occupant ran toward the nearby White House Hotel to get help. The owner of the town's garage was among the many skaters who were enjoying the hotel's large out-door rink. As Bertrand and the homeowner sprinted toward the lake, the garage owner quickly rounded up a handful of men. He stopped for tools at his garage then headed for the pier.

The depth off the end of the pier was one to three metres, and no one dared enter the water. The lake temperature on that cold clear night was enough to kill within a very short time. Minutes passed as half a dozen men worked frantically to attach a block and tackle to the hood of the submerged vehicle.

During that time, Léo Bertrand appeared to become more relaxed minute by minute. He talked calmly to bystanders, explaining that he had just stepped out of his car for a moment when it accidentally slipped into gear. He could do nothing, he said, as it slowly went over the edge into the lake. He then astounded them by asking opinions on whether or not the water would cause permanent damage to his car.

Police were on hand when the vehicle, with its lifeless passenger, was finally hauled out of the lake just before dawn. Three days later, on Christmas Eve, 1934, Léo Bertrand was arrested on suspicion of murder.

It appeared that many parts of Bertrand's story did not fit the evidence. Had the car simply rolled into the lake, it would have been recovered just off the pier. Instead, it was found more than 15 metres out, suggesting it was moving quickly when it left the dock. The inside handle of the passenger door was missing, preventing the passenger inside from opening her door. The handle was found in a toolbox in the trunk of the car. The existence of the newly signed double indemnity policy confirmed police suspicions that they were dealing with a homicide. Bertrand was charged with first degree murder.

The trial did not take place until almost a year after Rose's death. It lasted four days. After brilliant arguments by the defence lawyer, the jury found Bertrand not guilty. Within hours of his release, Bertrand contacted Eugene and demanded immediate processing of the insurance claim.

The $10,000 did not last long. Bertrand promptly bought a flashy new car to replace the old one, paid off his legal team, moved into a larger apartment across the river in Hull, Québec and had a stylish new wardrobe made to measure. Just six months after receiving the hefty insurance payment, the man who called himself The Tuxedo Kid was broke.

In mid-June 1936, a year and a half after he had buried his young wife, Léo Bertrand, accompanied by a male friend, walked into the Bank of Nova Scotia in Russell, Ontario. Both men were armed. Living in a sleepy little town a good hour's drive from Ottawa, Russell residents were not accustomed to armed hold-ups, but they were clearly not helpless. While his partner in crime waved a pistol in front of the teller's face, Bertrand, nattily dressed as always, opened the door to the manager's office. There he was met by a pistol held by a confident-looking manager. The two exchanged gunfire, and the robbers retreated, making their getaway in a waiting car.

They might have gotten away with the crime if not for Bertrand's acquisitive nature. Police discovered several scraps of torn paper in the alley behind the bank where the getaway car had been parked. The scraps were the remnants of a lottery ticket. When the scraps were fitted together, police started looking for the person whose name was on the back of the ticket. A Léo Bertrand of Dupont Street in Hull was soon arrested. Police picked up his accomplice a few days later. Eyewitness accounts, as well as fingerprint and handwriting evidence placed both men at the scene of the attempted robbery. As if that evidence wasn't enough, Bertrand and his accomplice bragged to a fellow inmate in the Carleton County jail about the hold-up. The inmate later testified against them. On October 23, 1936, they were found guilty of robbery with violence, and each sentenced to 15 years in prison.

For the next 12 years, Léo Bertrand's wardrobe was understandably less than haute-couture, as he served time, first at Kingston Penitentiary, then later at Saskatchewan's Prince Albert Penitentiary. He was released in 1948 and returned to Ottawa to resume his cabby career. Two years later, after moving to a better paying job in a drycleaning factory, he was promoted to plant foreman.

During his incarceration, Bertrand had come to the conclusion that his lack of formal education held him back from having the kind of lifestyle he longed for. He saved enough to apply for a mail-order degree from a fly-by-night American college. Two months and $50 later, Léo Bertrand had a parchment indicating he had a doctorate degree.

With the confidence and perceived status that came with his title of doctor, Bertrand became more officious and aloof than before. His job at the drycleaning factory soon became a sideline for him. Within a short time of receiving his bogus sheepskin, Dr. Léo Bertrand put up a shingle over the door of his rented office off Rideau Street indicating that he was open for business. His new line of work was psychotherapeutic counselling for emotionally distraught people.

With his professional offices, dashing clothes, a newly purchased Cadillac car and no way to comfortably pay for them, it wasn't long before Léo Bertrand found himself a rich girlfriend. Fifty-three-year-old Marie Charette, a wealthy and lonely Ottawa widow soon succumbed to the flashy doctor's advances. They married on September 3, 1951, despite the 15-year difference in their ages. Shortly after the wedding, the couple went to a notary to have their respective wills witnessed. They became each other's beneficiary. For the chronically overspent Bertrand and the well-heeled widow, it was a rather inequitable arrangement.

Before and after his wedding, Bertrand carried on an amorous relationship with a naïve schoolteacher named Ruth Bouchard, who knew nothing of Bertrand's marriage. In November 1951, just two months after his wedding, Bertrand took the young Miss Bouchard and her two sisters on a pleasant country drive to Lac Ste.-Marie, just north of Gatineau. He explained that he was renting a cabin and needed to take out some supplies before his upcoming vacation. They returned twice more to the cabin, both times in the company of the chaperoning sisters. Both times, the car was loaded with various items of camping equipment. One load contained two 20-litre cans of Varsol.

On Saturday, November 10, 1951, a group of young men from Lac Ste.-Marie were returning home from a party. Finding the traction poor on the snow-covered side roads, they stopped to put on tire chains. While stopped, they heard what they thought were gunshots. They assumed someone had fired at a skunk or other wild animal that came too close to their house. They resumed their homeward trip. They hadn't driven far when they saw a black Cadillac parked along the side of the road. Its engine was idling, and a man dressed in smart evening attire stood beside it.

The young men stopped, thinking the stranger had car trouble. To their surprise, the well-dressed man said that his wife had had an accident. He explained that a coal-oil lamp exploded, badly burning her hand and that their cabin was on fire. Thinking the man needed to drive his wife to medical care, the young men offered to take care of the burning cabin while he took her to the hospital. Bertrand became belligerent.

"Why would I need a hospital? My wife is in the cabin," he snapped. "I'm heading for the Hull police station to report the accident. And," he added, "don't bother going back there. There's nothing left." He drove off, leaving the young men gaping after him.

Bertrand did exactly as he said. While reporting the fire and the death of his wife, he was as calm and unemotional as if he was describing an everyday traffic jam. But his story sounded contrived to the Hull police, who were aware of the chequered background of the arrogant and officious man. They quickly involved the Québec

Provincial Police, who brought in some of their top investigators.

The cabin at Lac Ste.-Marie was cordoned off and examined in minute detail. The lamp, which Bertrand claimed had exploded, was found blackened but otherwise intact, its reservoir without so much as a trace of coal oil in it. The lamp, which had supposedly caused the fatal fire had never been used. On examination of the charred remains, police found that the body of the average-sized Marie had been reduced to what amounted to less than two kilos. There was so little of the woman's body remaining that cause of death could not be ascertained.

"She could have been strangled, shot or beaten to death," the coroner later testified. "No one will ever know."

Further evidence showed that the heat had been so intense that the woman's body had basically been cremated, a sure sign that an accelerant had been used. The discovery of empty Varsol cans near the scene confirmed the suspicions. Bertrand was picked up and charged with his wife's murder.

The trial lasted a week. Witnesses for the prosecution included experts from various disciplines and the young men who stopped to help Bertrand on the road. Jean Drapeau, who later became the flamboyant mayor of Montréal, was Bertrand's defence attorney. Despite his thorough research and skilful defence, he could not convince the jury to believe Bertrand's story. Forensic evidence alone was enough to incriminate his client, but Bertrand's neighbours, friends, and coworkers gave testimony that further pointed to his guilt. Shortly after his wedding to Marie, he bragged that soon he would never have to work again.

After delays caused by the presiding judge's fatal heart attack, Bertrand was found guilty of first degree murder of his wife Marie and sentenced to hang. He appealed but lost.

Léo Bertrand, 39 years old, was hanged from Montréal's Bordeaux Prison gallows shortly after midnight on June 12, 1953. The natty Tuxedo Kid made his final exit from this world clad in drab grey prison flannels.

CHAPTER ELEVEN

Albert Johnson
Mysterious Migrant
(circa 1897–1932)

It was February 17, 1932. Temperatures near the Arctic Circle hovered around −50°C —the kind of temperatures that made exhaled breath crystallize and exposed flesh freeze almost on contact with the frigid air; the kind of temperatures that made most people want to stay inside by a cozy fire with a hot rum toddy in hand. But that day, eight men on the ground and three in the air were bundled up against the harsh elements. They had no choice. They were after a killer.

It had been a terrible and gruelling seven weeks since they had started chasing the man they believed to be Albert Johnson. There had been no letup in the weather, and the man they were hunting was like a phantom—here one minute, gone the next. They had no idea what they were dealing with. But his accuracy with the guns he carried had already killed one man and seriously wounded another. If the rumours going around were true, he had likely killed many more. The Mad Trapper of Rat River had to be caught.

He came out of nowhere, this new trapper. Singular and solitary, he was a blue-eyed, fair-haired man of medium height, age around 35. With the build of a middleweight wrestler, and the attitude of a wounded cougar, he rarely gave anyone the time of day, let alone his name. In the Dirty '30s, along the wooded banks of the rivers in Canada's Northwest Territories, one man looked much like another. Hair uncut, faces unshaven, covered from head to toe to keep out the cold in winter and the relentless black flies in summer, men were identified by their camp setup, their voice or their walk.

When the stranger appeared along the river-bank that summer in 1931 and answered to the name Albert Johnson, the name stuck. But it wasn't a name the stranger had supplied. A local aboriginal man had heard that a seasoned white trapper named Albert Johnson was on his way to the area. No one by that name had shown up in town, and few white men without experience travelled alone. It was a logical assumption that this lone stranger was Albert Johnson.

After responding to the name, however, the stranger made it clear he neither needed nor wanted anyone's company. He kept to himself but was occasionally seen carrying his 90-kilo pack across the tundra looking for new locations for his traplines and when he came into town to purchase supplies. In Fort McPherson, where almost everybody lived a hand-to-mouth existence and strangers made friends quickly to assist in their survival, there were two reasons why the man they called Albert Johnson was unique. First, he didn't look like he wanted to make friends with anybody, and second, he was loaded with cash.

On the infrequent trips he made into the town to shop at the Northern Traders Limited store or the Hudson's Bay Post, he said little as he pulled carefully rolled bills from a tin can. He once paid out just under $1000 in large bills for a load of dry goods, traps and ammunition. Not long after, he purchased a canoe from a local man and paid cash for that as well. Each time people approached him, he kept his face partially covered or averted, said little and rarely looked anyone in the eye.

Despite his unusual behaviour, Albert Johnson received only passing interest from the Royal Canadian Mounted Police, which was already a presence in the Arctic. Because he was a stranger, RCMP officers asked him where he was headed and reminded him to purchase a trapping licence before establishing a trapline. They also asked him where he was from, since at this time their role included census-taking.

In a light Scandinavian accent, he told them he had come from the Prairies and had arrived in the Arctic via the Mackenzie River. The police were sure the latter was a lie, since one of their men had come upon him in the Peel River system on his way to Fort McPherson, but they didn't press the issue. Trappers and prospectors were notoriously close-lipped about their territories and, in the harsh world of the north, they had reason to be.

The RCMP decided Johnson needed watching but only for his own protection, since he insisted on doing everything without anyone's help or guidance.

After leaving the Fort McPherson area, Johnson was spotted several times during the summer of 1931 tracking* up the Rat River. He stopped en route at one of the many tent cities in the area, an area that was ominously known as Destruction City.

Johnson must have liked the general location. He built a cabin a full day's walk from the nearest neighbour, at a bend in the Rat River and on a rise that gave him an unobstructed view on all but one side.

It wasn't long before Johnson made his presence known. On Christmas Day, 1931, three trappers whose camps and traplines were already in place when Johnson built his cabin, trekked to the nearest RCMP post and filed a complaint that Johnson was springing their traps.

---

*tracking: moving a canoe upriver by walking along the shore pulling a line attached to the canoe; often used by wilderness travellers to navigate difficult, narrow or shallow waterways

Although it may seem like a child's prank to comfortable 21st-century people, springing a trap in the high Arctic in the 1930s was tantamount to attempted murder. Without meat to eat and pelts with which to buy provisions, men were left at the mercy of the wilderness. It was a serious crime.

The next day, the duty constable dispatched two officers into the Arctic chill to investigate. It took them two days of hard mushing* to reach Johnson's pit cabin. Pit cabins have nothing in common with anyone's idea of even a modest summer cottage. Johnson's residence was little more than a lean-to, consisting of a dug out area about the size of an average clothes closet, with a dirt floor about one metre below ground level, a slanted canopy of logs and boughs over-head, and a solid 1.3-metre-high door.

Sturdy as it was, it was more like a bunker than a dwelling in both size and comfort. It certainly gave Johnson the advantage he wanted when uninvited visitors came calling.

The first time RCMP Officers Alfred King and Joe Bernard came by, Johnson simply stayed inside and did not answer their knock at his crude door or respond to their questions about his neighbours' report. After two hours of patient waiting, King and Bernard decided they needed a search warrant and mushed the 130 kilometres to Aklavik. The duty officer there heard the story and decided the two men needed reinforcements.

---

*mushing: travelling via sled powered by a team of sled dogs

He rounded up two more constables to accompany King and Bernard back to Johnson's camp. The constables' second visit, with warrant in hand on New Year's Eve, was met with a clear message that they were not welcome.

As King approached the cabin, calling out first who he was and that he had a warrant, a shotgun blasted. King fell, seriously wounded. The others moved in close enough to provide covering fire as King crawled out of range. Johnson fired shot after shot, some narrowly missing the constables. Realizing King was seriously wounded and could die if they didn't get him to medical care, the officers abandoned the siege against the cabin and lashed King to the sled for the long trek back to Aklavik and a doctor.

With 130 kilometres of travelling just completed, the men and dogs had to summon every bit of strength and stamina they had to start out on the trail once more, this time with the dead weight of the wounded officer. Twenty hours later, after steady travelling over rugged, snow covered frozen ground in wind-chill temperatures that reached –60°C, they reached Aklavik.

King would live. The bullet had passed through his body at chest height, from one side to the other, missing his lungs by centimetres and his heart by a hairsbreadth. In top physical condition, King was back on his feet in three weeks. But while he was mending, a posse of eight constables, headed by Inspector A.N. Eames, was organized and dispatched as quickly as a 40-dog team and supplies were assembled.

By January 9, the posse was positioned in a semicircle around Johnson's shack on the few approaches available. The men were right out in the open on the riverbank. Johnson was inside: smoke from the chimney attested to that fact. Eames shouted that the officer Johnson had shot was alive and that he was not going to be arrested for murder. He said they only needed to talk to him about the sabotaged traplines. The answer they got was silence, then a gunshot.

The police officers attempted to approach the well-positioned cabin, but each time they were forced back by bullets. There was simply no way for them to reach it without putting themselves into the line of fire. Johnson kept up an extremely effective defence. The constables were aware of Johnson's situation and how it compared to theirs. He seemed to have an endless supply of bullets; he had food; he had a fire and access to wood from behind his shed; he was accustomed to the ruggedness of the traplines; and he knew the area. In contrast, they had limited food for themselves and their dogs; they were exposed, with only an open fire to keep them warm; and they were in an unfamiliar wilderness. But perhaps what played most on their minds was that Johnson had a motive to do what he was doing, and they didn't know what it was.

Back in Aklavik, they had checked as much as possible to find out if there were fugitives from the law in the area. There were none. There had been no robberies reported, no murders, nothing that would have made Albert Johnson react the way he had to the police officers. Nothing, that is, except cabin fever.

Had Albert Johnson been living so long in the woods alone that he had lost his mind? His behaviour certainly indicated it. Yet, his attention to detail in caring for his traps and his ability to survive out in the wilderness without anyone's help seemed to be sure signs that the man's faculties were intact. It made no sense, but it had happened. And whether or not they understood the behaviour, the RCMP had to deal with it.

About 9:00 PM, under cover of darkness and almost continuous gunfire from Johnson, one of the police officers got close enough to the cabin to lob a stick of dynamite onto the slanted roof. The explosion blew the smokestack off and collapsed the roof, but no response came from Johnson except for more gunfire.

The standoff lasted into a night that was increasingly cold. By 1:00 AM, January 10, the temperature had dropped to a deadly −50° Celsius. Johnson's gunfire was still strong and so was his persistence. At 4:00 AM, his persistence paid off. Uncertain of Johnson's mental state and concerned about their own survival, the posse left. Although burning Johnson out was an option, they rejected the idea. They worried that a crazed man might decide to go down with his burning home, and he hadn't done anything that they knew of to deserve that fate. They returned to Aklavik to find that the plight of the fugitive, newly dubbed the Mad Trapper of Rat River, was being broadcast on long-wave radios all over North America. It was the stuff legends were made of, and they were living it.

Officers sent back to the cabin a few days later found that their quarry had fled, leaving no trace of the direction he had gone. With additional supplies and reinforcements, a renewed effort began on January 14, 1932 to bring Johnson out of the woods alive. Trackers and woodsmen, both aboriginal and non-aboriginal, were recruited to fan out from the area of Johnson's cabin to pick up any sign of him.

On January 30, word came to their base camp that smoke from Johnson's campfire had been spotted. But a blizzard moved in quickly, and temperatures that had been hovering at −30° Celsius plummeted. It was clear the limited supplies would not go far for the 40 men involved in the search; a smaller group of men would move faster and more stealthily. Four well-trained men, two RCMP officers and two special aboriginal constables, equipped with a dog team and a radio, set off from the main group to apprehend Johnson. The police thought the standoff was nearing its end, but it was actually just beginning.

As the small group approached Johnson's campsite, the ever-alert Johnson was ready. All it took was the snapping sound of a twig that one of the trackers stepped on. In less than a heart-beat, Johnson opened fire at the sound. Both sides threw themselves into cover. After a two-hour standoff, Constable Edgar "Spike" Millen tried to rush Johnson's hiding place and was shot through the heart. The RCMP knew they were dealing with no ordinary fugitive. They knew they were hunting a killer—a killer who was so desperate that he might kill again.

On February 2, two days after Millen's shooting, a party of five headed again by Inspector Eames set out toward the Rat River area. This time they were monitored from the air by a Bellanca monoplane carrying two constables and piloted by WWI double ace Wilfrid "Wop" May.

For the next 16 days, the posse tracked Johnson. On February 17, with air backup and luck on their side, they found him camped along the Eagle River. As Eames approached with his party, he called out several times for Johnson to surrender. All he got in response was shot after shot of gunfire from an apparently crazed fugitive who would stop at nothing to keep from being taken alive. His shots popped so rapidly that it was clear he was using both hands, validating the rumour that he could shoot right or left with equal accuracy. Even after being wounded, he continued to return their gunfire and managed to hit and seriously wound one constable. It took several shots aimed straight into his dugout to stop the barrage of bullets. The next few minutes of silence told them that the Mad Trapper of Rat River was dead.

When they reached his body, they found that he had been shot at least seven times. His injuries included a massive thigh wound incurred when ammunition in his pocket exploded after being hit. The fatal shot was a bullet through the spine.

Once his body was returned to civilization, RCMP embarked on the huge task of identifying him. His personal effects included five pearls, five gold fillings that had not come from his own mouth and a packet of gold nuggets. His packs contained the usual survival gear and food but not one item giving a clue to his personality or identity. Several theories were put forward, but no definitive evidence came to light. Fingerprints turned up nothing. He was buried in an unmarked grave in Aklavik's Anglican Cemetery, his identity a mystery.

Albert Johnson was the subject of a massive manhunt that lasted 48 days. On foot, alone and existing off the land, he led his pursuers across dangerous and uncompromising terrain in blizzard conditions for 70 kilometres, shooting with the intent to kill anyone who got in his way. To this day, no one knows why.

Notes on Sources

Léo Bertrand

Smith. Barbara. *Fatal Intentions: True Canadian Crime Stories*. Toronto:
    Hounslow Press, 1994.

Hilda Blake

Kramer, Reinhold & Tom Mitchel. *Walk Towards the Gallows: The Tragedy of
    Hilda Blake, Hanged 1899*. Don Mills: Oxford University Press, 2002.
Redekop, Bill. *Crimes of the Century: Manitoba's Most Notorious True
    Crimes*. Winnipeg: Great Plains Publications, 2002.

Edwin Alonzo Boyd

Vallée, Brian. *Edwin Alonzo Boyd: The Story of the Notorious Boyd Gang*.
    Toronto: Doubleday Canada Limited, 1997.
Smith. Barbara. *Fatal Intentions: True Canadian Crime Stories*. Toronto:
    Hounslow Press, 1994.

Klaus Burlakow

Redekop, Bill. *Crime Stories: More of Manitoba's Famous True Crimes*.
    Winnipeg: Great Plains Publications, 2004.
Bourette, Susan. "A Tangled Tale", *The Toronto Globe and Mail*, May 20, 2003.
Editorial "The Con Man with a Triple Personality," *Irish Sunday
    Independent*, November 15, 2004.
Holliday, Bob. "Ex-official pleads guilty to robbery," *Winnipeg Sun*,
    May 16, 2003.
Owen, Bruce. "Bank robber jailed 8 years," *Winnipeg Free Press*, February 4,
    2004.
www.theolymipan.com/home/news/20040811/topstories/118653.shtm
www.cbc.ca/stories/2004/06/14/burlakow_plea
www.city.winnipeg.mb.ca/police/press/2003/feb03/20030215.htm

The Black Donnellys

Kelley, Thomas P. *The Vengeance of the Black Donnellys*, Toronto:
    Pagurian Press Limited, 1975.
————. *The Black Donnellys: The True Story of Canada's Most
    Barbaric Feud*. Toronto: Pagurian Press Limited, 1986.
Kelley, Thomas P. *The Black Donnellys*. Willowdale: Firefly Books, 1993.
Hendley, Nate. *The Black Donnellys: The Outrageous Tale of Canada's Deadliest
    Feud*. Canmore: Altitude Publishing Canada Limited, 2004.
Fazakas, Ray. *The Donnelly Album*. Toronto: Macmillan of Canada, 1977.
www.crimelibrary.com/classics.donnelly
www.crimelibrary.com/notorious_murders/family/donnelly
www.donnellys.com

Albert Johnson

Horwood, Harold & Ed Butts. *Pirates & Outlaws of Canada 1610–1932*.
    Toronto: Doubleday Canada Limited, 1984.

Macpherson, M.A. *Outlaws of the Canadian West*. Edmonton: Lone Pine
    Publishing, 1999.
North, Dick. *The Mad Trapper of Rat River*. Toronto: Macmillan of
    Canada, 1972.
North, Dick. *Trackdown: The Search for the Mad Trapper*. Toronto:
    Macmillan of Canada, 1989

Ken Leishman

Redekop, Bill. *Crimes of the Century: Manitoba's Most Notorious True
    Crimes*. Winnipeg: Great Plains Publications, 2004.
Robertson, Heather. *The Flying Bandit*. Toronto: James Lorimer &
    Company, 1981.
www.canada.com
www.playbackmag.com

Nick Lysyk

September 2002 through September 2004 various newscasts
"Ex-bank manager guilty of $16-M fraud," *Winnipeg Free Press*, August 31,
    2004.
"The insatiable appetite for stuff," *Winnipeg Free Press*, Vol 132, No 270.

Bill Miner

Anderson, Frank W. *Bill Miner, Train Robber*. Calgary: Frontiers
    Unlimited: 1963.
Dugan, Mark and John Boessenecker. *The Grey Fox: The True Story of Bill
    Miner—Last of the Old-Time Bandits*. N.P.: University of Oklahoma
    Press, 1992.
M.A. Macpherson. *Outlaws of the Canadian West*. Edmonton: Lone Pine
    Publishing, 1999.
Horwood, Harold & Ed Butts. *Pirates & Outlaws of Canada 1610–1932*.
    Toronto: Doubleday Canada Limited, 1984.
Paterson, T.W. *Outlaws of Western Canada*. Langley, B.C.: Mr. Paperback,
    1982.

John Schneeberger

Tetley, Deborah. "Violation of Trust: The Strange Case and Bizarre Crimes
of Dr. John Schneeberger," *MD Canada* (March/April 2004).
Manning, Lona. "Rapist, M.D.," *Crime Magazine: An Encyclopedia of
    Crime* (April 3, 2003).
Driver, Deanna. "Foreign Headaches," *The Medical Post* (April 19, 2000,
    Volume 36, Issue 15).
CTV News: October 2000 through November 2003 various newscasts
CBC News: December 2003 through June 2004 various newscasts
www.cbc.ca/stories/2003/12/04/schneeburger031204
www.mediresource.sympatico.ca/channel_health_news

Valentine Shortis

Friedland, Martin L. *The Case of Valentine Shortis: A True Story of Crime
    and Politics in Canada*. Toronto: University of Toronto Press, 1986.

GWEV Publishing Inc.

Angela Murphy

Angela Murphy is Angela K. Narth. She is a full-time writer with an extensive and varied background in education. She has held positions as university lecturer, public school administrator, and curriculum consultant before deciding to pursue a career in writing.

A published author, Narth has four children's books and several magazine articles currently in print. She is a freelance literary reviewer for the *Winnipeg Free Press* and the *Ottawa Citizen*. Her reviews have also been published in *Books in Canada* and *The Gazette* from Montréal. She is a member of the Writers' Union of Canada and the Manitoba Writers' Guild.